THE CAMBRIDGE REVISION GUIDE

GCE O LEVEL

ENGLISH

R. Glover, G. Rodway, P. Shirley and H. Toner

CAMBRIDGE UNIVERSITY PRESS
Cambridge, New York, Melbourne, Madrid, Cape Town, Singapore, São Paulo

Cambridge University Press
The Edinburgh Building, Cambridge CB2 2RU, UK

www.cambridge.org
Information on this title: www.cambridge.org/9780521644211

First published 2000
12th printing 2006

Printed in Singapore by C.O.S. Printers Pte Ltd

A catalogue record for this publication is available from the British Library

ISBN-13 978-0-521-64421-1 paperback
ISBN-10 0-521-64421-6 paperback

ACKNOWLEDGEMENTS

Cover image courtesy of Getty Images – Jack Hollingsworth

Introduction

This book has been written for all students of the English language who are preparing for public examinations. Although its title refers to the GCE O level, the contents are equally applicable to students studying for other examinations that contain elements of directed and continuous writing, comprehension and summary.

The writers are senior Cambridge examiners with over 50 years' examining experience between them, and even more teaching experience. All of them have been involved in training teachers how to prepare students for examinations, and how to mark scripts. Their work has taken them to Singapore, Brunei, Malaysia, Indonesia, Namibia, Botswana, Gambia, Zimbabwe, Argentina, Chile, Lesotho and Mauritius. They are familiar with the range of 'international English' spoken outside the UK itself, and sympathetic to the difficulties of learners in trying to master the oddities of the English language.

Now that the authors have turned their attention to students, they have set out clearly what the components of most formal examinations in the English language consist of and how learners can develop the skills that lead to success. They take students step by step through the processes, answering frequently asked questions, giving examples of work and explaining why students gained the marks they did. They also offer practice tasks for the student.

The book is written for you, the learner. Think of the writers as sympathetic friends who want very much to help you. You don't have to work your way through the book from the first page to the last. Use the contents list to find the parts that you know will benefit you most. Then use the rest to check your skills.

Cambridge International Examinations

Contents

Unit 1
Continuous Writing

Introduction

Whichever of the Cambridge International English Language examinations you take, you will be asked to produce a piece of *continuous writing*, i.e. to write a story, an explanation, a description or an argument, choosing your subject from a list that will be printed on the paper.

In your school or college you may know continuous writing by another name. You may call it a composition, an essay or, perhaps, a theme. It doesn't matter what you call it; a piece of writing as described above is continuous writing.

Here is some preliminary information:

❶ You will have about five or six subjects to choose from, depending on which examination you take.

❷ You will have about one hour to complete your piece of continuous writing.

❸ You will probably be advised to write between 350 and 600 words, but you are not expected to count the words and to remain rigidly within these limits.

Golden rule

The quality of your work is what counts – not the length.

To give you some idea of the subjects that are set in these exams, here is a list taken from recent Cambridge papers, including the instructions that are given at the head of the continuous writing paper.

Write on *one* of the following topics.

At the head of your composition put the number of the topic you have chosen. You are advised to spend about 60 minutes on this part of the paper and to write between 350 and 600 words. Total marks for this part: 40.

1. A noisy argument.
2. You were arrested because the police thought you were someone else. Tell the story.
3. A large water pipe bursts suddenly. Describe the scene, the reactions of those present and the after-effects.
4. If you had a problem, to whom would you turn for advice, and why?
5. 'Crimes are more often committed by men than by women.' If this is true, what can be done about it?

You now have some basic facts about the continuous writing paper. The next step is to go through the procedure you should follow so that you can produce a piece of writing that shows the examiner your work at its very best.

2 Choosing the topic

Your choice of topic could have a great effect on how well you do. You may be nervous at the beginning of an exam, anxious to get started and afraid that you will run out of time if you don't begin writing immediately, *but*:

Golden rule

Don't start writing until you are settled and sure.

The first thing to do is to read the *entire* paper slowly and carefully. Which of the topics gives you the best chance of writing a composition of the required length?

What would your answers be to the following three questions?

❶ Which sort of writing are you best at? You will have written practice compositions during your English course. Which were the most successful?

❷ Do you find it easier to write stories or descriptions than to construct arguments? Candidates who are not strong in English may find it easiest to tell stories or to write descriptions because they can move from event to event without having to follow an argument step by logical step.

❸ Are any of the topics close to something you are very interested in? If so, you may be lucky, but be careful! You might be able to write 200 very impressive words at the beginning. Can you keep it up for another 200–300?

You can safely spend at least five minutes making your choice. Don't worry if the candidate next to you starts writing furiously after a minute and a half. (S)he might be heading for disaster.

Keep cool!

3 Planning

After you have chosen your topic, you still have important work to do before you start writing, and that is to *plan* your composition.

Planning is very important, and in the examination you should spend about ten minutes on it.

There are various ways you can plan a piece of writing. We will now look at one method.

Mind map

This is a way of planning which involves making a diagram of your thoughts, showing connections and developments which you can use as a framework for your composition.

For example, suppose you chose question 4 from the list on page 4:

'If you had a problem, to whom would you turn for advice, and why?'

You could start by writing the two most important words from the title in little 'balloons' like this:

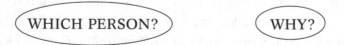

'Anchoring' your map onto the most important words in the topic will keep your plan focussed. In other words, it will stop you wandering off the topic as you make your plan.

You then 'expand' outwards from these two 'balloons', telling the reader something about:

- your chosen person
- your relationship with the person
- some details about the person, linking these with the reasons you chose him or her to be your adviser

You could add some examples of how you were given good advice, or how you avoided making a bad decision. Your 'balloons' might look a bit like this after you have finished your mind map.

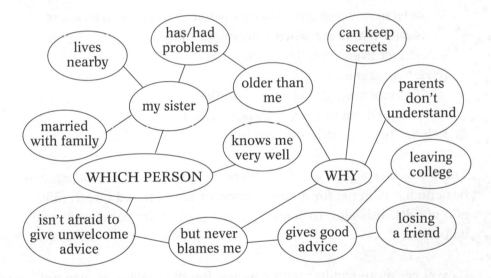

When you practise your composition writing, you may take a long time over your mind map. Don't worry about this, but try to speed up gradually so that by the time the exam comes, you are really confident that you can complete your mind map within the time available.

When it is completed, your mind map can be used to plan your paragraphs and to organise the shape of your composition.

Using the above map your plan might look something like this:

❶ Statement – I would turn to my sister.

❷ Describe her
   – age – older – married – has children – lives nearby
   – always been close to me
   – had problems herself when younger
   – give details

❸ Choose her because:
   – she keeps secrets
   – understands teenage problems better than parents/teachers
   – doesn't blame me when I do stupid things
   – is frank even when the truth hurts
   (give two examples)
      – stopped me giving up my studies
      – helped me to solve a dispute with a friend
❹ Rely on her – trust her – admire her

There we have a plan which answers the question on the paper, and has enough material for a composition of the required length (350–600 words). It is also, to some extent, a plan of the paragraphs you will write.

As you get more familiar with composition planning, you may not need a mind map to get you started, and you may go straight on to the paragraph plan. The important thing is to practise planning so that you can organise your thoughts before you start writing.

Practice session

Practise these first two steps by preparing mind maps and plans for the other four topics from the list of exam questions on page 4. Note how long it takes. Aim to complete each plan in 15 minutes. When you have written all the plans, keep them in a safe place — you will need them again. Show them to your teacher or to friends and ask for their comments.

You may find it easier to plan a story or a description of a series of events than to plan an argument or the presentation of your views on a topic. This is because the events you are describing provide a framework for you to follow, and lead you forward step by step in your writing. You may be tempted to think that a story doesn't need a plan but you would be mistaken. A story needs to be just as carefully planned as any other form of continuous writing. It is very easy to become tangled up in the events of a story unless you know before you start writing exactly what is going to happen in the story and how long it is going to take to write it. Examiners read hundreds of stories every year that start well but collapse after a few paragraphs because they have not been properly planned.

Getting started – the opening paragraph

Now that you have a plan, you can start writing, knowing that you won't run out of material. You will still have about 45 minutes of writing time and can use most of it in the production of the composition, unlike those who 'crashed in' and started writing immediately, and who may well have lost their way by now.

The first paragraph

One of the most difficult (and most important) steps in writing a composition is to get a good start. The first paragraph is vital in many ways:

- it informs the reader about the subject matter of the composition
- it sets the approach to the topic
- it gives the examiner the first taste of the writing skills of the candidate

Golden rule

The opening paragraph should show the writer at his/her very best.

Here are three openings to compositions on the topic which we planned earlier. Read them carefully, and decide which is the best (and why).

Remember the question title, 'If you had a problem, to whom would you turn for advice, and why?'

Piece 1

> Brr, Brr went my trusty alarm clock, and my eyes opened to see the sun casting its radiant glow through the flowered curtains of my bedroom. Outside, the birds sang to welcome me to a new day. I could hear the sounds of my mother as she moved about downstairs, preparing my delicious breakfast of fruits and cereals which would give me such a wonderful beginning to the day. I stretched like a kitten, and made my way to the bathroom where I took a long refreshing shower. As I was drying myself, I remembered my problem.

Piece 2

> If I had a problem I would not hesitate; I would go at once to my sister and seek her advice. She might not be particularly glad to see me – she is a very busy person – but it would be worth risking being scolded, just to have the benefit of her wisdom and maturity.

Piece 3

> The day had started normally enough. I got up as usual, did all the usual beginning-of-the-day things, and set off to school feeling reasonably happy. In other words, it had all the signs of a normal, perhaps not very exciting day. How was I to know that by the time the sun set, I would be running about trying to find someone to listen to my woes and to help me solve my problem. It was then that I turned, as I always do in a crisis, to my sister.

Piece 1

The English is quite good. There aren't many language mistakes. Some of the description is interesting. *But*:

❶ The paragraph has nothing whatever to do with the subject. It could just as easily be the first paragraph of a composition about a birthday party, a holiday or a wedding.

❷ The examiner will suspect that this paragraph has been prepared beforehand and is being served up regardless of the topic that has been set on the question paper.

So what will the examiner do? The examiner will not deduct marks, but will:

- note that the beginning is unsatisfactory
- give no credit for the language in the paragraph
- regret that the candidate has wasted time producing a paragraph that is not connected with the subject that (s)he has chosen to write about
- feel that the paragraph has distracted the reader from the subject (s)he thought was going to be discussed

Piece 2
This is the 'straight to the point' approach. No time or space is wasted. The reader is in no doubt what the composition is about and the writer makes clear that the paragraphs that follow are going to answer the question directly.

There is a great deal to be said for this approach. It does sound a little abrupt, perhaps, and might not suit the opening of a story where some background or atmosphere is necessary to bring the characters and events to life, but for this topic it is a good opening. The examiner is going to be quite impressed.

Piece 3
This is an interesting way to start the topic. It runs the risk (but avoids falling into the trap) of wandering off as the first one did. It cleverly contrasts the normality of the beginning of the day with the chaos at the end of it, and introduces the idea that the writer desperately needed advice before the day was over.

For this opening to be successful, however, it will be necessary to continue in the same vein, and to tell the story of the crisis, showing how important the sister's advice was, and why, therefore, the writer always turned to her. In other words, a good opening but with some risks involved.

You can see from these three examples how important the opening paragraph is. A piece of continuous writing can be 'made' or 'broken' by its first paragraph.

Practice session

Go back to the mind maps you made for the list of topics in Chapter 1. Write an opening paragraph for each of the topics. As you do each one, compare it with the three examples we looked at. Are you sure that you have avoided producing anything like Piece 1?

Golden rule

Don't ever write a prepared opening paragraph hoping that the examiner won't notice, or a paragraph that sounds good but clearly isn't on the topic set.

5 Length

Now that we have practised planning a composition and writing the first paragraph, we are almost ready to talk about the whole piece of continuous writing. However, before we discuss the details of what exactly is going to be assessed by your examiner, there are a few important points that we should clear up.

First, the length of your piece of continuous writing. Note that the instruction was to write 350–600 words. It is important that you understand the purpose of this advice:

- Examiners *do not* spend time counting the words of a composition so that they can deduct marks if you stray outside the limits.
- Advice is given about the word limit, because over the years, we as examiners have noticed that if a candidate tries to write too much, more and more mistakes are made as tiredness sets in, and the mark we can award gets lower and lower.
- On the other hand, a very short piece of writing is unlikely to do justice to the subject, and that lowers the mark too. This is one of the reasons why planning is important – so that you don't run out of ideas, or ramble on without a plan.

In other words, you are most likely to produce your best work if you aim to write within the limits given on the question paper, and you have planned accordingly.

But don't worry if your essay is a little short or a little long.

The examiner has more important things to judge than the mere length of the writing. If you take your time to choose your topic and plan carefully, there should be no need to worry about length. Don't waste time counting the words and recording the total number at the end of the composition, or, worse still, inventing a number that you think will impress the examiner – it won't!

You might find it helpful, however, when you are practising your continuous writing, to note how much you can reasonably write in 45 minutes. If you find it difficult to develop your plan into a 'finished product' in the time available, that shows that you need more practice, and that you must use every minute available during the exam to the very best effect.

Golden rule

Take the advice on length seriously. But don't waste time counting words or worrying about the exact length of your composition.

6 Standard English

You will find that the expression 'standard English' is often employed when describing the language you are expected to use in this examination. Many students (and even some teachers!) seem to misunderstand what this means.

We are *not* expecting you to try to copy the language of one of the great British or American writers of many years ago, or to attempt a grand kind of language that you may have come across in your reading.

The English we are looking for has the following qualities:

❶ Most important of all, it communicates clearly to the examiner, and to an English speaking person in any part of the world.

❷ It obeys the rules of spelling, punctuation and grammar that are accepted and practised in the English speaking world.

❸ The vocabulary (words) used is suitable for people who are expected to read the piece of writing.

This last point needs, perhaps, a little more explanation. You will have come across several different kinds of English in books, magazines, films and TV. If English is only one of the languages that you use, you may not realise fully the difference between formal and informal English.

The examination is a fairly formal occasion. In general (except when you are writing, for example, a conversation in a story) the English you use should be formal.

It should *not* contain:

- slang
- expressions which might be acceptable in a conversation between friends, but which are out of place in a piece of writing intended to demonstrate the writer's ability to use standard English correctly

Here is an example of a paragraph which would cause the examiner to doubt whether the candidate knew how to write accurate standard English.

> The party was made up of four guys and three chicks, all looking cute and cool. They were gonna really really swing today cos exams were over and school and all that crap stuff was dead man dead.

That is the sort of language you might well come across in films or on TV and you might not realise how 'slang-ridden' it is. Such language would do severe harm to your mark if you used it, as, sadly, some candidates do, in a standard English exam.

Practice session

> Re-write the above paragraph, replacing all the slang expressions with standard English.

Your final version should look something like this:

> The party was made up of four boys and three girls who all looked attractive and fashionable. They were going to enjoy themselves (today) because exams had finished and the boring school work was over and forgotten.

Golden rule

Don't copy the language of comics, TV soaps, 'cops and robbers' fiction, or books written long ago. Use English that you feel comfortable with and which will be easy for your reader to understand.

7 Relevance

You will probably have heard the term 'off-topic' writing or 'irrelevancy'.

We mentioned this problem when we discussed opening paragraphs earlier on. We said then that an opening paragraph which had nothing or very little to do with the subject of the composition would not be given credit by the examiner, and the candidate would have wasted valuable time producing it. But what does the examiner do if the whole composition wanders off the topic?

The answer is that we have a definite procedure and it is as follows (*please take note!*):

❶ If the examiner feels that the composition is a perfectly honest response to the topic which has somehow *unintentionally* wandered off the subject, the final mark will be reduced a little.

❷ However, if the piece has obviously been learnt by heart before the exam, or is probably a 're-hash' of an essay on a different topic written in class before the exam, or if the topic has been deliberately 'twisted' to enable the candidate to write about something not on the question paper, (s)he will be *penalised* very heavily indeed and can certainly say goodbye to any chance of a high grade.

Golden rule

Don't ever try to avoid the purpose of the examination (to test your ability to write standard English) by writing a prepared composition or by deliberately twisting the title.

8 Assessment objectives

Before we start considering compositions as a whole, you need to know exactly *how* your composition will be marked. There are all kinds of myths and misunderstandings about how your final mark will be arrived at. You should learn how marks are allocated, so you will be aware of what examiners look for when they decide what mark you should have.

❶ They don't read your composition and then deduct marks for mistakes you have made.

❷ They don't allocate a certain number of marks for spelling, a certain number for punctuation, etc., and then add up the bits to arrive at a final mark.

❸ They don't just read through and give a mark depending on whether they like the story, find the description interesting or agree with your opinions.

Marking process

Marking is actually quite a scientific process, and works like this:

❶ The examiners have a list of skills which go together to make a successful piece of writing. They call these *assessment objectives*.

❷ They then draw up a description of the level of performance in these skills that corresponds to each of the grades in your examination.

❸ They choose sample compositions in each grade to act as examples.

❹ They exchange scripts with each other during the time they are marking your examination work, to make sure that they are all applying the same standards.

❺ They re-mark many scripts, particularly those which have just missed an important grade.

Examiners are very anxious that you should get fair treatment and that you are properly rewarded for the skills you have developed and shown in your examination work.

Nothing would please them more than to be able to give high marks to every script that they read.

Examiners are on your side. They want you to do well!

In the next few chapters we will go through these assessment objectives one by one and show you what examiners are looking for and how you can help yourself to do well in the examination.

9 Communication

To begin with, just pause for a moment and think of the main purpose of any piece of writing, whether it is a love letter, a newspaper article, a legal document – or an examination composition. Its first purpose is and must be *communication*! It might be a simple message left at home when you go out. For example, 'Gone to buy a newspaper – back in 20 minutes.' No problems here. The reader will, in a real sense, 'get the message.'

However, not all short messages are as clear as that one. There is a story of a boy who left a message asking his parents to leave him a note telling him whether he could spend a large sum of money on a new pair of shoes. He later found a note from his mother which said, 'No price too high.'

What did that mean? Did it mean that whatever the price, he should go ahead and buy the shoes? Or did it mean that the price was too high, and that he should *not* buy them?

We don't know what the boy did, but I don't think the mother could complain too much if he rushed out and bought the shoes. After all, the message was not clear. In other words, communication was not satisfactory.

So, the first thing examiners look for when they read an examination composition is clarity of communication. Does the candidate transfer to the readers information, opinions or descriptions which are clear and precise? Do we know exactly what he/she means? This is our first assessment objective.

Grade descriptions

Let's look at some of our grade descriptions where they refer to communication:

❶ For Grades A–D your writing *must* convey meaning clearly. The reader (examiner) must be able to read your essay at normal speed and know exactly what you are saying. There must be no doubts in his/her mind.

❷ At Grade E, meaning is not in doubt, but it may be necessary to read rather slowly to be sure that meaning is understood.

❸ At the top of the 'U' grade, meaning is established but there may be moments when the reader isn't quite sure what is being said.

❹ Below the top of the 'U' grade, meaning starts to disappear, and the examiner, sadly, will not be able to give many marks.

Here are three short pieces of writing, each from a 'real' candidate who took the exam in the past.

Imagine that you are an examiner and have to place each of these pieces in either Grades A–D, Grade E or Grade U. Consider *only* the level of communication achieved – don't bother about other things that might strike you as good or bad.

Piece 1

> When someone is in trouble the later should always a person to advise. Hence in my case when I had a problem I always goes to incle place to solve my problem. My uncle has fourty years old, he lived with wife and at Curepipe two children. He was tall black hair with blue eye and dress, very smart. He was very complensive and dislike people was deaf ear. He like to collection stamps and occupied his garden, it is a serious man.

Piece 2

All this took place on a Monday morning during recreational hours at school. At this hour of the day, the school yard was bustling with activities. However, in a corner of the yard a quite noisy argument was going on between two upper class girls, namely Pam and Mary. I was on my way to the canteen when I noticed the feverish argument that they were having.

Piece 3

In my opinion, sometimes it happens that some children they do not pay attentions to what they parents are going to ask them to do but they think that they have grown now enough and it is not important for them to listen at their parents advise. Sometimes they might be at the write path but it might be in the contrary too. This is so particularly for the case of a children of about fifteen years old.

What did you think of those pieces? Remember, we are judging them only for their clarity of communication.

Piece 1

You will probably agree that although some sense emerged, there were several moments when we were not quite sure what was being said (or meant!). For example, was the uncle tall, or was his hair tall (i.e. long)? What does 'complensive' mean? Did he dislike deaf people or did he turn a deaf ear (i.e. didn't listen to) people he didn't like? You probably found other confusing bits as well. The meaning is sufficiently unclear here to give the examiner very grave doubts, even at this early stage, whether the final mark could go above Grade U.

Piece 2

An easy one to assess. There is never a shadow of a doubt about meaning here. Communication is crystal clear. The examiner may well find fault when (s)he applies other assessment objectives, but the communications test is passed with flying colours. This piece is likely to score between Grades A–D.

Piece 3

Did you find this one a little more difficult to place? You must have noticed that the candidate makes many mistakes through the piece, but we are only looking at communication. Could you understand it all? Did the mistakes come between you and an understanding of what the writer was trying to say?

The answer is that only very occasionally is there any doubt. Despite the mistakes, nearly all of the piece communicates clearly. It is a stronger piece of communication than Piece 1, but not nearly as clear as Piece 2. It might just get Grade E, depending on our judgement of other assessment objectives.

Do you see, therefore, that in your own writing, your first job is to make sure your intended meaning is conveyed to your reader without any confusion whatsoever? This will mean choosing your words carefully, making sure the punctuation helps the reader (remember the expensive shoes!) and watching out for sentences that might be misunderstood.

Golden rule

Always ensure that you are making things easy for your reader. Check your writing carefully for mistakes that might be confusing.

If you look again at the three examples of communication above, you will see that in the weakest one communication was unclear, because of the many mistakes the candidate made. Candidate 2 did not make many mistakes, so communication was clearer. The writing of Candidate 3 was clear when it was reasonably accurate. The lack of clarity occurred because of mistakes.

There are, of course, many different kinds of mistakes you can make when writing in English. By avoiding them, and by doing some positive things, communication can be made clear – or crystal clear – giving you a higher mark.

There is no space in a revision book of this kind to go through all the possible grammatical errors that you might make when writing a composition. The best way to keep improving is to make sure that whenever you write a composition, you get someone to check it for you and to point out your mistakes. In this way you will gradually eliminate your errors and produce better work.

Look now at the various things you will be doing when you write an essay:

- using words
- organising words into sentences
- punctuating sentences
- paragraphing
- spelling words correctly

This list is a simplified version of some of the most important assessment objectives we referred to earlier on. We can now go through each one to see how we can improve our continuous writing.

10 Vocabulary

Any piece of writing consists of words, each of which means something – it conveys a message. For communication to be clear, you must use words that convey to the reader, as exactly as possible, the information that you intend.

To begin with, let's consider the word 'walk'. We all know what this means, i.e. to travel on foot. If we know this word, we can convey a message which will tell the reader that someone (or something) is moving on foot.

Consider the following sentences:

- The soldier .... across the parade ground.
- The couple .... along the beach.
- The baby .... across the room.
- The drunkard .... along the street.
- The injured footballer .... off the pitch.
- The old man .... into his house.
- The student .... to catch his bus.

Now, put the word 'walk' into each of the gaps. The sentences work perfectly well, don't they? In each case the reader will understand that the people in the sentences moved (using their feet).

Think of some other words which mean almost the same as 'walk' but which would give the reader a clearer picture of *how* the person moved.

Practice session

Look at the following list of words and fit one into each of the above sentences to give the reader a clearer picture.

strolled	marched	limped	rushed
toddled	hobbled	staggered	

How did you do? You probably said that the soldier marched, the footballer limped or hobbled, the baby toddled, etc.

By using these words instead of 'walk', you added 'colour' to your writing and gave your reader a much clearer picture.

CAUTION

Before you use a word, you must be sure you really know what it means. Think of the confusion you would have caused if you had said that the soldier toddled or strolled, or that the baby marched. If you didn't know 'toddled', it would have been much better to have said 'walked'. At least both you and the reader will know what it means!

Now consider another example:

A young man is intending to propose marriage to the girl of his dreams, and thinks that it would be a good idea to tell her how beautiful she is before he 'pops the question'. He starts off by saying, 'You are very long and thin.'

He then wonders why the girl bursts into tears and rushes off in a sulk. What had he done wrong?

What he meant to say was, 'You are very tall and slim.' The words are very similar, but there is a world of difference between the ways the lady is likely to react.

Or consider the word 'yellow'. It would be perfectly reasonable to say that the sun is yellow, a crown is yellow, a Buddhist monk's robes are yellow. But how much more exact the picture will be if you use the word 'golden' to describe the sun and the crown, and saffron, if you know the word, to describe the monk's robes!

Golden rule

Try to use words which give an exact picture to your reader – but never use a word if you are not perfectly sure what it means.

If English is not your first language, you will obviously want to build up your knowledge of English words and to learn how to use them with precision. You can best do this by reading novels, newspapers, non-fiction books, e.g. travel stories. But always try to find writing that is in standard English. The English of light romantic novels is fine if that's what you like – there's no need to read novels of the 19th century – but avoid writing that uses slang.

Ask your teacher to recommend some good books that you might enjoy reading and which will build up your 'word power'. There is plenty of excellent writing to choose from. What about some of the best detective fiction, or some travel stories?

Practice session

Now try your hand at being an examiner again. Read the following three passages and rank them in order of merit. Look only at two factors – communication and vocabulary. How exact, rich and precise is the description? How clear is the communication?

Piece 1

Dear Jenny,
I hope you are well. Here, most of the people are having bad coughs. Last Tuesday when I was going to school, there was a very big storm. It was raining very hard. I wore my raincoat and took my umbrella. On the road there weren't many people. Buses were rare. All the shops were opened and there were a lot of people in them buying things they needed if the storm got worse. There were only a few students at school. We had the assembly in the hall and we didn't do much work.

Piece 2

Last week, our island suffered a terrible storm. Unfortunately, our house is positioned in such a way that it is vulnerable to strong winds. These winds, and the heavy rain that accompanies them, cause the soil on the hillside to move, and come to rest against the back wall of our house. Although a small barrier wall has been constructed, heaps of soil always accumulate, destroying plants and small shrubs that my parents try to grow.

But last week, we had more to worry about than lost shrubs. We were warned that this storm would be a violent one – strong enough to threaten our lives if we didn't take proper precautions, and so there was a flurry of activity all day while we were making our house watertight, ready for the monster wind that was rushing towards us.

Piece 3

Last Sunday saw us in a ecstacy of perambulation as my kinsfolk and I exercised our corporate effort in a supreme attempt to ward off the evil demons that were rushing tempestuously towards us in the ineffable shape of the demonish hurricane. My elder sibling of the feminine gender was lamenting the incipient deprivation of her choicest rose bush, whilst my mother was welcoming the arrival of her constant companion in woe – the Saturnine migraine.

What is your verdict here? Remember, you are judging only the use of vocabulary and the success of the candidate in communicating clearly with the reader.

Piece 1

This is a very simple, straightforward piece of writing. Communication is absolutely clear. The reader/examiner will 'get the message' with no difficulty at all.

But what about the message? The letter to a friend described a very frightening experience that the writer had had – a major storm that disrupted life in the country and threatened the lives of many people. However, the writer is not able to convey any of the danger or excitement of the occasion. S(he) can use only simple words to describe the experience and therefore cannot bring it to life. The examiner would give credit for the clarity of the communication, but would feel that the candidate would have to be able to use many more 'precise' words to earn a very high grade.

Piece 2

Again the communication is clear. So far, then, we can compare it with Piece 1. But very soon we see that the writer is able to use words that convey the excitement and the anxiety of the great storm; words like 'vulnerable', 'accumulate', 'threaten', 'flurry', and 'watertight'. These words all add 'colour' to the picture being painted by the writer, and they are all used correctly so that they fit together to make the description come alive. We can say, therefore, that communication is not just clear – it is precise, accurate and vivid.

Piece 3

I wonder what you thought of this one. There are certainly some long words in it – do you know what they all mean? Is this a very clever writer? Or a rather unwise one? It is quite clear that this candidate has learnt a large number of very complicated English words, and is determined to use them. Some of them s(he) understands quite well, but (s)he has only a vague idea of what others mean. The words are flung onto the page hoping that the examiner will be impressed and award high marks.

Examiners often go back to basics and ask themselves the first question, 'Does this passage communicate clearly?' The answer, sadly, is 'no'. 'Perambulation' is a long word for 'walking' and is hardly used nowadays. In any case, the writer doesn't intend to talk about walking; s(he) wants to speak of people rushing around preparing for the storm. Why not say 'rushing around'? It would be simpler, clearer to the reader, and give the exact 'picture' intended.

Why say 'kinsfolk', when 'family' is meant? 'Corporate' is the wrong word altogether, and I'm sure that the writer has no clear idea of what 'ineffable' means. The result is muddle and confusion. The long words don't help the reader. No clear picture emerges, as it did in Piece 2, and the simple clarity of Piece 1 is not achieved either. This is a poor piece of writing because the writer is trying to show off his/her knowledge of long English words without understanding them or considering whether they are the right words to use for this description.

My order of merit is, therefore:
Piece 2
Piece 1
Piece 3

Practice session

Look again at Pieces 1 and 3. With Piece 1, try to 'beef up' the description by changing some of the simple words for others that make the picture more vivid. Don't change the sentences – just some of the words.

However, remember you are trying to make the picture clearer – don't try to use 'clever' words and spoil communication.

With Piece 3, replace some of the long but 'wrong' words with others that are simpler but which help to make meaning clear. You may need a dictionary to check what some of the writer's long words mean. You may be very surprised!

Golden rule

Never try to impress your examiner by using words which sound clever but may not mean what you intend. Use words which you are sure about. Use words that give the exact picture you are trying to convey. Often the simple word is the best one.

Punctuation

Just imagine what it would be like if no punctuation marks existed. Words would be strung together in a senseless jumble, and you would have to decide where to pause, and for how long. Questions and exclamations would be the responsibility of the reader – not the writer – and there would be no guarantee that any two readers would come to the same conclusions.

At worst, communication would be threatened, or might even break down altogether.

Practice session

Read the following short passage, which is written without punctuation. You will certainly see what we mean when we talk about communication breaking down. Try to punctuate the passage so that meaning is absolutely clear.

two boys met after school one day they were intending to go shopping in a new mall but we havent asked our parents one boy said they might be angry mine wont mind replied the other boy its going to rain and we shall get wet insisted the first boy but we have umbrellas replied the other boy theres a bus coming lets get on it we can decide what to do on our way but im not very sure i want to im going home said the first boy the second boy looked disappointed

Your version should look something like this:

> Two boys met after school one day. They were intending to go
> shopping in a new mall.
>
> 'But we haven't asked our parents,' one boy said. 'They might be
> angry.'
>
> 'Mine won't mind,' replied the other boy.
>
> 'It's going to rain and we shall get wet,' insisted the first boy.
>
> 'But we have umbrellas,' replied the other boy. 'There's a bus
> coming. Let's get on it. We can decide what to do on our way.'
>
> 'But I'm not very sure I want to; I'm going home,' said the first boy.
> The second boy looked disappointed.

It would be very rare to find an examination candidate missing out
punctuation altogether, but we often find scripts which are quite
good in some ways but that let themselves down by inaccurate or
careless punctuation.

Here are some of the most important points to bear in mind when
writing your essays and checking them for errors:

❶ If you are going to use direct speech (actual conversation) make
   sure that you know the rules. It's very easy to make punctuation
   errors when writing direct speech.

❷ You *must* use a full stop at the end of each sentence. It's no good
   using a comma and hoping your examiner won't notice.

❸ Make sure that you learn the rules regarding apostrophes. There are some tricky ones that you should revise. If you want to use, for example, 'can't' or 'won't', make sure that the apostrophes are in the right place. Make sure that you also know the difference between 'it's' and 'its'.

❹ If you use question marks or exclamation marks, make sure that you use them only after real questions or exclamations; and *never* use a string of exclamation marks to emphasise a particularly dramatic piece of information.

Practice session

Read the following extract from a 'real' examination paper. There is a number in brackets every time a punctuation error occurs. See if you can identify each mistake and correct it. If two bracketed numbers are printed next to each other, it means that there are two mistakes for you to correct.

When I opened my eyes (1) I knew that the weather would not be glorious today, (2) I switched on the radio and listened to the news at 7am, (3) I was horrified!!! (4) (5) Its (6) going to rain cats and dog's (7) today (8) (9) I wailed. (10) Mum (11) (12) I called, 'may I stay at home today (13) (14)

'No (15) certainly not,' came the reply (16)

'But, Mum,' I protested (17) (18) everyone else will stay at home (19) I cant (20) be the only one there, (21) And in any case (22) Im (23) frightened, (24) even the cat won't go out today. Look at the way its' (25) swishing it's (26) tail. I'm, (27) not going. (28) (29) Well (30) see about that (31) Ill (32) give you just two minutes to be dressed and out of the house (33)'

Did you manage all of the corrections? The correct punctuation of each error is listed below. Check carefully. If there is anything you don't understand, be sure to ask your teacher for help.

1.   Comma needed. It helps to break up the passage a little for the reader.

2.   Full stop needed. This is the end of a sentence – a full stop is essential.

3.   Full stop again. You might just be able to use a semicolon here, but a full stop would be much safer.

4.   *Never* use a string of exclamation marks. You could possibly use one exclamation mark here, but a full stop would be better.

5.   Although the narrator is speaking to him/herself, it counts as direct speech. You should therefore start the speech on a new line and insert speech marks (' ').

6.   This is one of the oddities of punctuation. 'Its' (without the apostrophe) means 'belonging to it'. To shorten 'it is' you need to say 'it's'.

7.   Remove the apostrophe – 'dog's' means 'belonging to the dog'. You don't mean that here.

8–9. A speech ends here, so you must place a comma after the last word spoken and close the speech marks (in that order).

10. Speech begins, so you need speech marks (' ') here.

11–12.   Speech ends, so you need a comma followed by speech marks.

13–14.   Two more mistakes here. A question mark is needed after 'today', and you must close the speech marks.

15. Comma needed.

16. Full stop. The sentence ends here.

17–18.   A comma is needed after 'protested' and the speech marks must then be opened.

19. You definitely need a full stop here. A comma would definitely be wrong. A sentence has ended and the speaker is heading off in a new direction.

20. The abbreviation of 'cannot' must be written as 'can't'. The apostrophe replaces the letters of 'cannot' that are left out in the abbreviation.

21. You must never follow a comma with a capital letter. In this case you have the choice of changing 'And' to 'and' or of putting a full stop after 'there' and deleting 'And', then starting the new sentence with 'In any case... '.

22. A comma would be helpful here.

23. Another abbreviation. It must be written 'I'm' with the apostrophe in place of the missing letter. When a writer refers to him/herself the 'I' must always be a capital letter.

24. You could use a semicolon here. However, if you are not sure about semicolons, a full stop would do perfectly well (followed by a capital 'E' for 'Even', of course).

25. Another variation on the error we dealt with above (6). When the meaning is 'it is', the apostrophe must go between the 't' and the 's' – 'it's'.

26. Yet another version of the mistake (6) . In this case the meaning is 'belonging to it', so 'its' without the apostrophe is the correct version.

27. This comma is not needed here and might confuse the reader. Remember that unnecessary punctuation counts as an error; always know *why* you are punctuating.

28. The speech comes to an end here, so the speech marks must be closed *after* the full stop.

29. Another speech begins, so speech marks must be opened again. The speech must begin on a new line.

30. Another abbreviation, so the apostrophe is needed and goes where the letters of 'we will' are missed out. The correct version is 'we'll'.

31. A full stop should be placed here; it is the end of a sentence.

32. Yet another abbreviation. Correct version is 'I'll'.

33. The speech ends, so you should place a full stop after 'house' and before the closing speech marks.

Golden rule

Check your punctuation carefully before the end of the exam. Read to yourself (silently!) what you have written. Are the pauses in the right places?

12 Organising sentences

So far, we have dealt with choosing the correct words, punctuating so that the reader can be clear about the meaning, and making sure that communication is as clear as possible. We now come to another important aspect of continuous writing that your examiner will pay a great deal of attention to when s(he) assesses your work.

To begin with, look at these two very short pieces.

Piece 1

It was a Monday in June. It was early in the morning. The school was quiet. No one else had arrived yet. Today was an important one. Our exams were beginning today. I was very nervous. I had tried hard. I had revised for several hours each night. I felt ready. I was determined to do well.

Piece 2

It was early on Monday morning. As no one else had arrived yet, the school was quiet and deserted. Today was very important for me as it marked the beginning of our examinations. I had revised hard, staying up late each night revising, because I was so anxious to do well. I felt confident that I was well prepared, but I was still very nervous.

Do you see in which ways the two pieces are the same and in which ways they are very different?

- Both describe the same scene and the feelings of the writer.
- Both communicate clearly.
- Both use vocabulary which is simple but accurate.
- Both are correctly punctuated.

However, the examiner would not give each passage the same mark. In fact, there would be quite a large gap. Why?

The first piece is written in very short jerky sentences, causing the reader to receive the information in tiny 'bites'. If this had been a piece of writing 400 words long, the reader would have become very tired of the jerks long before the end.

The second piece is much more pleasant to read, despite using almost the same vocabulary and communicating the same pieces of information, because the longer sentences allow the information to be conveyed smoothly, linking up the various bits that go together to form the complete picture.

Golden rule

Avoid writing a long series of short sentences. Use your sentences to link ideas together so that the reader is carried smoothly from one idea to the next.

However, it is no good writing long, shapeless sentences that will probably confuse the reader.

Look at this sentence, for instance:

When I arrived at school, I was the first one there because it was very early on that Monday which was the day on which our examinations were going to begin for which I had prepared carefully by staying up late at night because I was anxious to do well, and now I felt well prepared and ready to do well in the exam but I still felt very nervous.

What a mouthful! The reader would be praying for the end to come long before s(he) had finished wading through all those words. To convey this information clearly and efficiently, a minimum of three sentences is probably required:

- to set the scene
- to explain the importance of the day
- to convey the writer's feelings

In Piece 2, five sentences are used, more than the minimum, avoiding jerkiness on the one hand and lengthy confusion on the other.

It might help to think of the reader/examiner reading your essay as though s(he) was eating a meal. If the sentences are too short the effect is rather like trying to use chopsticks for the first time – a great deal of effort is involved but only a tiny bit of food is gained at each attempt.

If, on the other hand, the sentences are too long, the food is like a dish of spaghetti in unskilled hands (or spoons) – the individual pieces are so long that eating the meal becomes a desperate attempt not to have spaghetti all over one's face, the tablecloth and the floor – again, dissatisfaction! The most satisfying meals are those which can be eaten in reasonably sized bites, big enough to taste and small enough to go into the mouth without causing a mess. Sentences, like food, should be served up in bite-sized pieces — not short and jerky, and not long and 'indigestible'.

Golden rule

When you plan your sentences, think of the chopsticks and the spaghetti. Don't starve your reader – and don't choke him/her!

However, writing a good composition is more than just deciding to write the whole thing in middle-sized sentences. We must now go on and consider another important aspect of sentence construction – variety.

Read the following paragraph. It is an extract from a 'real' examination essay describing an argument at school.

> Some of their friends tried to calm them, but the situation became worse. Both girls started insulting each other. Some of the words I caught were very insulting and extremely hurtful. Some of the replies were worse than that.

In many ways, this extract shows a good piece of writing, but look at the first few words of each sentence. They are:

- Some of their…
- Both girls started…
- Some of the…
- Some of the…

Three of the four sentences start the same way, with the same words. This is usually a bad idea. Though repetition can be used deliberately to achieve an effect, the reader will feel this is a clumsy way of writing. The above paragraph would have been better if the writer had varied the structures a little. For example:

> Although their friends tried to calm them, the situation became worse. The girls started shouting at each other. Insulting and hurtful words were used; even worse were some of the replies.

Here we have some variety of structure, which will be more likely to keep the interest of the reader, and to make the description more lively. A few words here and there have also been changed to remove repetition of words.

Golden rule

> As you write, try to vary the length and type of the sentences you use.

You can also use sentence variety to achieve a particular effect: to create tension, for example, or to give special emphasis to the point you are making in an argument.

Now read the following paragraph.

> When he entered the room it was dark – not just dark, but pitch black. As his eyes adjusted to the gloom, he could just make out the figure of a woman seated in an armchair near the fireplace. Slowly he walked nearer. She didn't move. When he was quite close to her, he noticed that her head was slumped forward and her arms were hanging loosely over the sides of the chair. Suddenly a feeling of dread came over him. Trembling, he placed his hand on her cold neck, trying to detect a pulse. There was nothing. He looked closer and saw the ugly red stain across her throat. She was dead.

Do you see how the author has built up tension by using the very short sentences 'She didn't move', 'There was nothing', 'She was dead', to convey dramatic information?

However, the writer does not only use short sentences to achieve effect. The longer sentences, whilst giving vital information, also provide the passage with a smooth flow which is interrupted by the short, dramatic sentences.

Golden rule

> Use sentence variety as well as appropriate vocabulary to achieve the effect you want.

Finally, before we leave the very important topic of sentence construction, we will look at another paragraph from an O level composition written recently. Read it carefully, paying special attention to the shape of each sentence. Do you notice anything special about these sentences?

> There were only four people in the team and they were trying to find the hidden path. There were two men and two women and they were faced with a battle against time. The rains would start soon and then their journey would be impossible. They were well equipped and were led by an experienced explorer. They were determined to succeed this time and to earn the 40 000 dollar reward. They knew that the odds were against them and that no one expected them to come back triumphant. Some people thought that the journey was too dangerous and that they would all be killed. Their honour was at stake and they were determined to prove their critics wrong.

What did you notice? There are no language errors – no punctuation or spelling mistakes. Communication is clear. The words used paint a clear and quite vivid picture. But no examiner would give it the highest grade. Why?

Go through the paragraph again, circling or underlining the word 'and' every time it appears. How many circles/underlinings did you get? You probably counted nine. That in itself doesn't mean much, but look at the way the sentences are constructed.

They are all built in the same way – two statements linked together by 'and'. What is wrong with that? There's nothing wrong in using that structure once or twice in a paragraph; but if you use it again and again, you produce a monotonous effect that is likely to cause your reader to lose interest, and would certainly harm your mark in an examination.

That is not all, however! Now read the paragraph once more, this time circling the first three words of each sentence. Then write out the words you have circled in the form of a list.

We get:

- There were only...
- There were two...
- The rains would...
- They were determined...
- They knew that...
- Some people thought...
- Their honour was...

Do you see? Not only are the sentences all of the same shape, but they all start in the same way, using mostly 'There', 'The', 'They', or 'Their' as their opening words. This will increase the monotony and cause your examiner to question whether you are capable of varying your sentences in type, length and structure in order to make your writing clearer and more interesting.

Practice session

Rewrite the paragraph, telling the same story, using more or less the same words, but varying the sentence length and type to make the story more vivid and interesting. When you have written your paragraph, test it by counting the 'and's and making a list of the first three words of each sentence.

Here is a version that you might like to 'test'.

> Only four people, two men and two women, were in the team
> trying to find the hidden path. Theirs was a battle against time. Soon
> the rains would come, making the journey impossible, despite their
> excellent equipment and experienced leader. They were determined,
> however, to succeed. Although few people expected them to return
> triumphant, with many predicting that they would all be killed, the
> prospect of the 40 000 dollar reward drove them on. Moreover,
> even though they knew that the journey was dangerous, their
> honour was at stake. Their critics must be proved wrong.

You will see that, in this paragraph, both sentence length and type
are varied. The information is the same as in the original passage,
but it is presented in a way that is likely to be more attractive to the
reader – and more impressive to your examiner!

Golden rule

Keep checking the types and lengths of the sentences you are
using. Are you sending your reader to sleep?

13 Spelling

There is no doubt that some people find spelling extremely easy – they never get anything wrong. Others find that they have difficulties even with fairly simple words.

It is, of course, impossible in a revision handbook to teach you how to spell. What we can do, however, is to give you some hints and suggestions as to how you might improve your spelling, and an exercise or two so that you can check if your spelling is cause for concern.

❶ Most spelling mistakes that occur in continuous writing examinations are caused by carelessness, and not by a real spelling problem on the part of the candidate. When you are writing quickly in an examination, it is easy to make mistakes. The first hint, therefore, is to check your spelling carefully before you hand in your paper at the end of the examination.

❷ Whenever you do a piece of continuous writing, get your teacher – or anyone who can spell better than you can – to underline each word that is spelt wrongly.

❸ Make a list of these words, spell them correctly and try to learn a few each day. You may find at first that your list will grow longer and longer, but don't give up. After a while, if you stick to your daily learning programme, you will find you have trouble with fewer and fewer words.

❹ When you have reduced your list to the really troublesome words, write them on a card and carry it around with you. Look at the card whenever you have a spare minute or two – between lessons, on the way to school, on the way home, just before you go to sleep at night, or just after you wake up in the morning.

❺ Finally, you will have reduced your list to a few words that for some reason you always spell wrongly. Keep trying to get them right, but when it comes to the exam, don't use them. Find other words that mean more or less the same thing, and which you know how to spell. Use them instead.

For example:

> Her mother shouted, 'Come here *imediatly*.' ('imediatly' is wrong.)
> So instead say: 'Her mother shouted, 'Come here instantly.'
>   or 'Come here at this moment.'
>   or 'Come here straight away.'

You have communicated the information you wanted to convey, and have avoided making a spelling mistake.

Golden rule

In an examination, avoid using a word which you find difficult to spell. Use another word or words which mean(s) the same thing and which you know how to spell.

Practice session

Now let's find out whether you have a spelling problem. In the following passage, there are 20 spelling mistakes. They are words which some candidates in our exams find difficult. Rewrite the passage, correcting the spelling mistakes.

It was definately not going to be a good day. My mother's ancient vechile had a flat tyre, and nothing could be done imediately to mend it. No one knew how the dammage had ocurred although we suscepted the little boy next door, who had been showing more interest in the car than we thought was neccesary. On one ocassion we had caught him trying to open the car door.

I lay on my bed, gasing at the cieling, and hating the thought of having to walk all the way to school, and probably recieving a lecture for being late.

'It's too far,' I grumbled to myself, 'and their are dark clouds in the sky. Suppose I got wet and cought a cold. I might miss my crusial chemistry exam next Teusday. I staid up late too nights running, learning about the methods of making industrial alchol. I don't want to waist all that effort.'

The correct version is:

> It was DEFINITELY not going to be a good day. My mother's ancient VEHICLE had a flat tyre, and nothing could be done IMMEDIATELY to mend it. No one knew how the DAMAGE had OCCURRED although we SUSPECTED the little boy next door, who had been showing more interest in the car than we thought was NECESSARY. On one OCCASION we had caught him trying to open the car door.
>
> I lay on my bed, GAZING at the CEILING, and hating the thought of having to walk all the way to school, and probably RECEIVING a lecture for being late.
>
> 'It's too far,' I grumbled to myself, 'and THERE are dark clouds in the sky. Suppose I got wet and CAUGHT a cold. I might miss my CRUCIAL chemistry exam next TUESDAY. I STAYED up late TWO nights running, learning about the methods of making industrial ALCOHOL. I don't want to WASTE all that effort.'

How did you do?

If you got 15 or more of the words right, you probably don't have to worry much about your spelling. But always check your writing before you hand it in. If you failed to find several (or most!) of the incorrect words, you probably need to follow the learning method outlined on page 46.

14 Paragraphs

Many pieces of continuous writing that are in several ways quite good lose marks because of poor paragraphing.

There are three main weaknesses which we come across:

❶ No paragraphs at all. The writing is presented in one solid lump. If it was a piece of food we would choke. We would have to bite through it and reduce it to chewable pieces!

❷ 'Mini' paragraphs – compositions which have a new paragraph for almost every sentence. The bites are so small that we can hardly taste them.

❸ 'Casual' paragraphs. They begin and end for no obvious reason – perhaps because the writer thinks that the paragraph being written is long enough, and that it is about time to start a new one.

All of these approaches to paragraphing will damage your continuous writing mark. Paragraphs are, in fact, a form of punctuation, dividing the writing into manageable pieces, and leading the reader step by step through the description, story, explanation or argument.

A good paragraph has some important characteristics:

❶ A paragraph is complete in itself. It deals with a definite part of the story, or step in the argument, or point in the explanation. This is usually summarised in a topic sentence that normally – but not always – comes at the beginning of the paragraph and tells the reader what the paragraph is to include.

❷ A paragraph, however, must not stand alone like an island. It must be linked by 'bridges' to the paragraph before it (if there is one) and to the paragraph that follows it.

❸ The best compositions show variety in paragraph length so as to make the writing more interesting and vivid, in much the same way as a good writer varies his sentence length and type.

Practice session

Read the following extract from a composition on the topic, 'Are school rules really necessary?' We have numbered the paragraphs so that we can refer to them in our discussion, but they are, of course, not numbered in a normal composition.

1   Many people argue that school rules are not necessary. We are, after all, almost adults and know very well how we should behave. Our parents have taught us good habits and, when we were younger, they punished us if we misbehaved. There is no need, these people say, for a long list of rules and regulations. One rule would be enough: 'Always think of the welfare of others and the reputation of the school.'

2   This all sounds very reasonable, but I have grave doubts whether it would work. Think of the likely chaos that would arise in a school with no rules. If there were no rules for moving around the school, there would be 'student-jams' every time we changed lessons. Pupils would not wear their uniforms with pride, damaging the school in the eyes of the local community. Times for using the library or club rooms would not exist, and no one would know when they were available.

3   But that is not all. Think of the problems a new student would have, not knowing what he or she was allowed to do and when. It is perfectly possible that such a student, having to decide what was and was not acceptable, would behave in a way that was highly inconvenient to other students.

4   This picture of freedom is misleading. As teenagers, we don't need silly rules which tie us down unnecessarily, but we do need a framework within which the school can operate efficiently and fairly, protecting the rights of pupils to a good education, and the school from criticism from outside.

5   We all want our school to be held in high esteem by those being educated there and by those outside. Let us keep our rules – they are good for us!

Now look carefully at the paragraphing of this extract. Don't worry about other characteristics the piece might have. For this exercise we are concerned only with the paragraphing.

This candidate has done his paragraphing quite correctly. Bearing in mind the characteristics of a good paragraph that we listed above, let's examine the example. You will notice firstly that each paragraph is a complete unit. Each one deals with a distinct aspect of the subject:

- Para 1 – Arguments against school rules
- Para 2 – What would happen if rules were abolished
- Para 3 – Problems for new students
- Para 4 – The kind of rules that are needed
- Para 5 – Conclusion – let's keep the rules

Secondly, each paragraph contains a sentence that summarises the subject matter of the entire paragraph (the topic sentence).

Here they are:

- Para 1 – 'Many people argue that school rules are not necessary'
- Para 2 – 'Think of the likely chaos... in a school with no rules'
- Para 3 – 'Think of the problems a new student would have'
- Para 4 – 'We do need a framework within which the school can operate'
- Para 5 – 'Let us keep our rules'

Thirdly, the paragraphs are very well linked. Links can be of two sorts:

1. A word or phrase that refers back to the previous paragraph and leads on to the new one. There are several examples of this technique in the extract:

● Between Paras 1 and 2   –   'This all sounds very reasonable,
                                but…'
                                (leads on to new paragraph)

Between Paras 2 and 3   –   'But that (subject matter of Para 2)
                                is not all.'

Between Paras 3 and 4   –   'This picture of freedom (school
                                without rules) is misleading.' This
                                link doesn't quite work because it
                                refers not to the previous paragraph
                                (Para 3) but to Para 1. The reader
                                might be a little confused here.

2. The link can be a logical one, that is to say, carrying on a train of
   thought started in the previous paragraph. For example:

● Between Paras 4 and 5. The end of Para 4 – 'protecting… the
  school from criticism from outside' links with the beginning of
  Para 5, 'We all want our school to be held in high esteem.' This
  continues the idea started at the end of Para 4, and uses it to
  form a conclusion.

If you are writing a story, the sequence of events will often act as a
link. However, you should always look for a word or phrase which
will cause the reader to glance back at the previous paragraph and
to feel that the story is continuous and not a series of jerks.

Sometimes, a simple word or phrase can act as an effective link.

For example:

● 'However' (modifying some information in the previous
  paragraph)
● 'That was bad but worse was to follow' (moving the reader on
  and asking them to make a comparison between events)
● 'On the other hand' (presenting the second half of a description
  or statement of opinion)
● 'Then' or 'Next' (linking events, *but* don't use this link too often
  or your writing will become a monotonous list)

Finally, the paragraphs are varied in length, with the final paragraph short and emphatic to drive home the writer's opinion and conclusion.

Golden rule

Take your paragraphing seriously. Make your paragraphs complete in themselves but with links forward and back.

15 Handwriting and presentation

You may wonder whether we award marks for good handwriting – or deduct marks for bad handwriting – when we are assessing your continuous writing. The answer is that we don't. Indeed, we try to avoid being influenced one way or another by the quality of the handwriting. Handwriting is not one of the assessment objectives we listed earlier in the book.

However, it is to your advantage to present your work in a neat and orderly way, so that your examiner can read it at normal speed and never be in doubt about what a word is, how it is spelt, and whether you have used the correct punctuation marks.

Helping your examiner to read your work is a wise precaution! Here are some of the things you can do to help your examiner:

❶ Use a black ball point pen. Light blue on thin paper is often very difficult to read.

❷ Very small handwriting is hard to read even if it is very neat. If your handwriting is small, try to increase its size slightly.

❸ Don't try to cram too many words onto one line. Reasonable spacing makes for easier reading.

❹ If you want to cross something out, just draw a single line through it. Don't use liquid paper and then try to write over it. This usually makes a terrible mess and pages of your script tend to stick together.

❺ Make it clear where a new paragraph begins. Do this by indenting (leaving a space on the first line before the first word of the new paragraph).

16 Subject matter

So far, we have talked mostly about the language you use – how you can make your writing more accurate, more vivid and better organised.

However, none of these things are of much use unless you have something to write about. In an examination, of course, you are bound by the topics on the question paper, which is why subject choice is so important. Once you have chosen your topic, you have to decide upon your approach to the subject. Perhaps we can help you a little here.

When we set the continuous writing topics, we spend a lot of time trying to find subjects that candidates might be interested in writing about. This is quite difficult. Our exam papers go all over the world and it would be very unfair to set a question about mountains or a snowstorm, when many of our candidates live in low-lying islands in the tropics.

What we do is to find subjects that will be of interest regardless of where the candidate lives, and that usually means asking you to write about yourself – your life at home, at school, or among your friends; or perhaps to tell a story which we hope will be set in an area well known to you; or to express an opinion about a problem that you, as a teenager, are likely to be concerned about.

We are not trying to find out how much you know about a subject. It is not crucial that you get your facts right. We don't penalise candidates who think that New Zealand is situated between France and Norway, and we don't get offended when you write, 'She was an elderly woman of thirty-five'.

We don't expect you to imagine you are someone living outside your own experience. Many candidates seem to believe that writing as a New York traffic cop, an American soldier in Vietnam, or a beauty queen in Paris, will impress their examiner. Sadly, this is usually not the case. All too often, such compositions turn out to be half-remembered versions of TV programmes, probably not relevant to the topic, and using language that is only partly understood.

We are not asking you to express opinions that you think your examiner will agree with. If we ask for your opinion about something, we are happy to accept what you say, regardless of whether we agree or not. There are no extra marks for sparing your examiner's feelings, and nothing is deducted for having a teenager's view of life.

We hope that you will:

❶ Write as yourself. You are a teenager living in a country that most examiners have never visited. Your life may not seem particularly interesting to you, but it is certainly of interest to your examiner.

❷ Use your imagination as much as you like, but try to set your stories and descriptions so that you can describe what is familiar to you.

❸ Tell us about your joys and sorrows, your hopes and fears, your happy moments and the very occasional (we hope!) bad days. Tell us about your home, your family, your school, your friends. Build them into your stories; your writing will be much more interesting.

❹ You can be quite sure that your writing will be treated with great respect by your examiner. We may enjoy laughing *with* you on some occasions when your writing amuses us, but we will never laugh *at* you.

So, when you choose your subject, there is no need to 'go outside' the things that are familiar to you. If you want to write an adventure story or a love story, go ahead, but set it within your own experience or imagination. Never serve up someone else's ideas or material – they are second-hand and stale.

Golden rule

When you write, be yourself. Use experiences, settings and ideas that are familiar to you and that you understand.

17 Final touches

We have now been through the main features of a piece of continuous writing that will decide the mark that an examiner finally awards.

If you try to apply the *golden rules* that are given with each chapter, you will have a good chance of improving your writing and gaining the best mark possible in your exam.

One final piece of advice – a *'super golden rule'* –

Golden rule

Always leave yourself enough time at the end of the exam to check your work thoroughly before you hand it in. You are sure to have made mistakes which there is still time to correct.

Having made yourself an expert at continuous writing, you will now repeat the process with directed writing. Good luck!

Unit 1 — Further practice

If you have gone carefully through Chapters 1–17 of this book, you will have a good idea of what constitutes a good piece of continuous writing, which would give you the best chance of getting high marks in your examination. However, we can't leave it there.

What you need between now and the examination is regular practice. It would be very wrong, incidentally, to provide model answers for you. Continuous writing is a personal thing – everyone is different. Your writing should be a message from *you* – not an attempt to reconstruct someone else's story or ideas.

The more often you practise the skills you learnt in Chapters 1–17, the more likely your writing will improve.

You will find, below, a list of composition titles from recent Cambridge exams. They all come from papers actually set in the last few years.

Use this list to choose practice compositions. You should write one as often as possible. Aim to write at least one composition per week leading up to the examination. Do more than this if you only have a few weeks to revise.

In the first week, choose a title from List A, in the second week, from List B, and so on. When you have done one from each list, go back to List A and start again.

Here are the titles:

List A (Argumentative topics)

1. 'Young people have more problems than adults.' Do you agree?

2. 'It is ridiculous for a brave person to risk death helping a fool.' What do you think of this opinion?

3. 'Nowadays, there is little difference between the amateur and professional in sport.' What are your views?

4. Is population control necessary?

5. 'The computer is more a menace than a blessing.' What do you think?

6. 'Work hard, play hard.' What do you think of this piece of advice?

7. What are your opinions of traditional and modern dress?

8. Should physical education and games be compulsory activities in school?

List B (Descriptions – events)

9. Describe how local people reacted when a useful shop was demolished and houses built instead.

10. Write a description of any fireworks display or 'light' display that you have seen.

11. Write about a public occasion where two people have very different opinions about what is taking place.

12. Write about an occasion when you found yourself having to deal with an emergency.

13. You were called upon to take someone's place in a public performance at the last minute. Describe what happened.

14. What was the most important social event that you attended in the last year?

15. Describe a local wedding.

16. Describe the funniest event in your life so far.

17. Describe an occasion when a small fire went out of control.

18. Describe a day you spent in strange surroundings.

List C (Stories)

19. Write a story based on the phrase, 'Don't worry – it may never happen.'

20. Write a story based on *one* of the following:
    a) You were on a journey with someone who was suddenly taken ill.
    b) 'We were amazed when we heard how lucky John had been.'

21. 'It was obvious that she had never intended to keep her promise.' Write the story.

22. 'It is probably too late, but at least we can try.' Write the story.

23. Write a story on *one* of the following:
    a) An unfair punishment.
    b) 'He had been hungry, dirty and completely without hope. Now there was a chance of a new life.'

24. Write a story based on *one* of the following:
    a) While a doctor was away, a young, unqualified nurse treated a patient and things went wrong.
    b) Someone who refused to listen to the good advice of a teacher.

25. Write a story about a rich man who unexpectedly lost all his wealth.

26. Write a story on *one* of the following:
    a) A race against time.
    b) 'I had practised saying it a thousand times, but when the moment came, I just couldn't open my mouth.'

27. 'I had the world all to myself that early morning. The countryside as I walked through it was deserted and still.' Continue the story.

28. Write a story based on *one* of the following:
    a) 'When I was left behind, I was distressed.'
    b) 'I didn't know what happiness was until...'

29. Write a story based on *one* of the following:
    a) 'The situation became more tense as the crowd gathered.'
    b) 'As he searched, he opened the drawers of the desk and found...'

List D (Description — people and places)

30. Describe a new teacher you have had.

31. Describe your grandparents.

32. What do you think your country will be like in ten years' time?

33. Describe a popular person in your age group.

34. Describe interesting features of an area of your country far away from a big town.

35. Describe a very old person who is well known to you.

List E (Your opinions)

Write about:

36. ... some of the things that make you proud of your country.

37. ... the problem of choosing the right career.

38. ... 'my kind of music'.

39. ... wasted opportunities.

40. ... justice.

41. ... jealousy.

42. ... dangers on the road.

43. 'Time seems to stand still or to go much too quickly.' What are your experiences of this?

44. How do other nations influence your country?

45. The advantages and disadvantages of being an only child.

List F (General titles)

46. Write about 'seeing things'.

47. If you were offered the chance to visit any country in the world, where would you go, and why?

48. What were you afraid of when you were a child?

49. Write about this subject: 'Spies'.

50. Write about this subject: 'The wind'.

Although the titles have been divided into lists, that doesn't mean you have to respond according to the list headings. It is perfectly possible, for example, to write a story when responding to a title under a 'Description' heading, and many of the 'Your opinion' titles give you an opportunity to respond in several different ways.

Remember – provided your response is clearly relevant to the title, and you are not 're-hashing' material that is not your own, you may respond to the titles in any way you choose, unless you have been given precise instructions in the title. For example, when you are asked to write a story or to give your opinion on a particular issue, you *must* do so.

When you have chosen your title, go step by step through the
process of composition writing, as described throughout Unit 1 of
this book, as follows:

1. Choosing the topic:
    *   Are you fairly sure that you can write about 400 words on
        the topic you have chosen?
    *   Can you see the 'direction' your writing might take? If it is a
        story, do you know how it is going to end? If it is an
        argument, can you see what the conclusion might be?
    *   Stop for a moment and think carefully. Don't waste time
        moving to the next step if real doubts are beginning to arise.

2. Give yourself a time limit. For the first few practice
    compositions, allow yourself plenty of time – take, say, twice as
    long as you will be given in the exam. As you get nearer to the
    exam, cut the time down until you are within the time limit.

3. Now start planning. Are you going to use the mind map
    (page 7)? If so, remind yourself how it works. Does it suit the
    topic? Does it suit you? If it doesn't, don't use it. It is only one
    way of planning a composition.

4. Work out the parts of the argument, description or story that
    are going to be covered in each paragraph. Look again at the
    plan on page 8. Remember that there should be enough detail
    to enable you to write without having to keep stopping because
    you aren't sure what to say next. Don't start writing until you
    are happy with your plan.

5. Now for the opening paragraph. In the early stages of your
    practice you may wish to write several drafts. Practise until you
    can get it right first time.

    You will obviously want to avoid the flowery but irrelevant type
    of opening, but are you going straight into the topic? Or are
    you going to start with an introductory but *relevant* paragraph
    as described in Unit 1?

6. When you have written your opening paragraph, read it carefully. Is it what you want? Is your examiner going to be impressed? Is it the right type of opening for this particular composition?

7. When you are happy with your opening paragraph, you can start writing your composition. Keep referring to your plan. Don't change it unless you suddenly have a new idea that can safely be inserted without disturbing the general 'shape' of the composition.

8. As you complete each paragraph, scan it to make sure that you are sticking to the plan and that you haven't made any serious errors. If you spot a mistake, correct it there and then. Don't put it off till you have completed the whole composition.

9. Choose your words carefully. Ask yourself whether you are saying exactly what you want to say. Are you sure you know the meaning of the words you are using? If you aren't, don't use them. Choose a simpler word that you *are* sure about. Words are your weapons – make every shot count!

10. Avoid slang at all costs. Remember that words or phrases that might be fine in a conversation may not be suitable for a written composition. If you use slang, your examiner may doubt your ability to write accurate English.

11. What about the sentences you are using? Are you thinking about the impression they will make on your reader/examiner? Are you consciously trying to vary the length and type of sentence used in order to convey information or ideas vividly? Do you find yourself using the same type of sentence over and over again? Look particularly at the first three words of each sentence. Do you find the same pattern repeating itself?

12. Be careful with your spelling. If you are not sure of how to spell a word, try to find another one that means the same and which you know you can spell correctly.

13. Punctuation is *very* important, particularly the full stop and the comma. Make sure your sentences are separated correctly with a full stop at the end of each sentence.

14. Check for errors and correct them quickly. Are you making corrections neatly?

15. Make sure your handwriting is easy to read.

Keep the above list at your side as you write. When you have finished, and checked carefully, leave your composition for a while, preferably overnight. Then we can come to the next stage in our practice – *assessment*!

Assessment

By assessment we mean applying the assessment objectives (*see Chapter 8*) to a piece of continuous writing so that a mark can be given which reflects the quality of the composition.

In a real examination, your work will be sent off to be assessed by an examiner appointed by the examination board. While you are practising, however, it is useful to chart your progress by assessing the standard you have reached in each piece of writing you do.

You will find in the following pages 8 short pieces of writing. Compare the quality of your writing with these pieces. Of course, as they are very short you can only consider the language used – vocabulary, sentence structure, spelling and punctuation. The pieces are too short for you to come to any conclusions about the strengths and weaknesses of the content of the story, description or argument.

Which piece most resembles your work? Why? Now look at the grade above the one where you have placed your work. What could you do to move up one grade – or two?

Don't worry about Grade U9(i). This grade is awarded to writing that is too weak to qualify for Grades A–E and acts as an indication of how near the piece is to qualifying for Grade E.

When you have come to a final conclusion about the standard you have reached, read your composition carefully, making some notes about weaknesses so that you can bear them in mind when you try your next title.

File your compositions in the order that you write them. Re-read them from time to time and see how you are improving. Get your parents or a friend (preferably one who is good at English!) to read your compositions, and discuss them.

Be prepared to take criticism and learn from it!

Good luck.

Piece 1

Because of my fear. I accidentially pull up the joystick that move the aircraft and it fly! If fly higher and higher and I try to control the plane but it become much more difficult to handle. I screamed and shouted for help but it is to late. I have seated on the aircraft for 15 minutes long ine the sky. I have difficulty to hear because of the air preasure. I realised that the aircraft have not enouth fuel when the engine suddenly stop.

[Grade U1 – almost E]

Piece 2

The minutes I told my class-mates that was no relief teacher… before I could finished my announcement all of them jumped up and shouted "hooray!" Quickly I ordered them to keep quiet, and sit down.

At first, they obeied. But my class well known "monkey" – Shakir started to make noise. He tried to disturd a girl who was sitting just beside him. He pulled he hair and laughed. Not to show that she was weak, she scolded him in a loud voice. her act was unespected by all of the classmates included me. I was shocked for a minute then I tried to solve the problem. I asked Shakir to appologice but he disobey me. Anyway I tried to persuied that girl to sit down and don't quarrel with him.

[Grade E]

Piece 3

This morning with my hands full of bags, I went to the Railway
Station to catch my train at 10.00am. I went there with a cab. To my
surprise, when I just stepped my feet outside the cab I could see a
terribly very huge crowd inside and outside the Railway Station. I
paid the fair, as I said to myself, 'Oh no! I'm a dead meat. I am
going to face a big crowd.'

As soon as I got myself into the crowd, I could smell millions of
odour smells that were really horrible. I could not help myself to get
rid of that because my hands were full with luggage, so I just
squeezed myself between two Chinese people and managed to pull
myself out of the crowd onto the bridge to the Railway Station. I
was lucky as I have booked the ticket to Alor Setar. So I didn't
bother to queue up for a ticket. In fact, there was a long queue at
the ticket's counter.

[Grade D – just!]

Piece 4

The first and main thing I would do if I had a lot of money is donating. I would donate some of my money to the orphanage and old folks' home. I would also help the poor so that they can lead a happy life and have enough food to eat.

The next thing I would do is to help my parents who are the closest person to me. I would try my best to support them and therefore I would ask them to stop working. I would make them happy and grant all their wishes.

I have always wanted to travel around the world. If I had a lot of money, I could make my wish come true. I would then be able to visit Europe and the United States of America. I would meet many people of different races, languages and cultures.

[Grade C]

Piece 5

The new house was a few blocks away from where we used to live but it was very much smaller than our double-storey bungalow. We had no choice but to minimize our furniture as the new single-storey semi-detached house was unable to accomodate them. Almost everyone was reluctant to move out at first, but we had no choice. My elder brother's education expenses was quite taxing for my father since the Malaysian Ringgitt had depreciated so badly against the US dollar. Besides, my father needed the money to help finance his company's losses. The timing was also right according to him, as the value of the property was quite high.

[Grade C – nearly B!]

Piece 6

The sound of the large vehicle's engine interupted the song I was listening to on the radio. Looking out the window of the house which I will no longer occupy I saw the lorry pull up on the driveway. Boxes of furniture, clothes, household appliances and other belongings were then loaded onto the lorry. I was quite surprised to see the boxes fill the vehicle to its maximum capacity. I thought that with so many old belongings either given away or left behind, the boxes would not even fill half the lorry.

[Grade B]

Piece 7

I walk down the narrow hallway and touch the single mantle. Mummy used to cram pictures of the two of us there, but now that they have been removed, it's just mother's dusty old mantle; dusty like this house. Faded spots show where pictures used to hang, even though the pictures themselves are long gone. Dents in the carpets, where fluffy couches used to sit, linger on even though no chairs are there to dent them any more.

This old house holds so many memories. I remember the tireless piano lessons in front of the beautiful picture window, and seeing the sun beams upon the magnificent flower garden up front. I remember the huge oak tree in the back yard and the swing hanging from it. Sherry and I spent many years trying to climb to the top. I say 'trying' because Mummy always caught us before we even reach the fifth branch! We found and nurtured many a baby bird up in that tree.

[Grade A]

Piece 8

At around the age of four I experienced temporary separation from my family members. The incident lingers in my mind because of the utter desolation that engulfed me when it occurred. My parents, older sister and I were shopping in a crowded departmental store in Singapore. The number of people and the array of goods on display quite overwhelmed me and I gave in to curiosity at last. Letting go of my mother's restraining hand, I wandered off to stare in fascination at something or other. Before I knew it, I was lost. I gazed in total disorientation at the shoppers milling around me but saw no familiar faces. I resorted to the only method a child knows to get attention — tears. The rest of the incident is vague. I only remember being reunited with my frantic family some time later. I also recall a friendly face and a gentle hand leading me — most probably a passer-by who noticed the tear-stained face of a lost little girl.

[Grade A+ — full marks!]

Unit 2
Directed Writing

Introduction

By following the advice in the unit on continuous writing, you will probably have made a successful start to your English examination. This means you are ready to build on that success when you come to the directed writing task. (You may know it better as guided writing or functional writing or writing for a purpose).

For directed writing, in most Cambridge Examinations Syndicate examinations, you are allowed half an hour to complete the task, and you are told to write between 200 and 300 words. This is only half the time given for continuous writing and an answer of approximately half the length is generally expected.

Furthermore, directed writing is marked out of just half the marks set aside for continuous writing (normally 20 instead of 40). All this might give you the idea that it has only half the importance of continuous writing, but this is certainly not the case. Doing well in this second part is vital to gaining a good mark for the whole paper, so you must give directed writing a proper sense of importance. A really successful candidate on the composition paper will be someone who does well on *both* continuous writing and directed writing.

Golden rule

Make sure you leave the right amount of time to complete the directed writing. It is just as important to your overall success as continuous writing or any other part of the exam.

2 What is directed writing?

In the Cambridge syllabus it says that directed writing is, 'A task based on a situation described in detail, in words or diagrams'. In the directed writing task or guided composition, you will be given very clear instructions in order to complete a writing task. You are being directed towards your writing in two ways:

- you are being guided very clearly as to *what* you have to write
- you are being told just as clearly *how* to set out the answer

This type of question requires you to concentrate on every bit of information you are given. Let's look at an example.

Your principal received the following letter:

Dear Sir

As I was walking near your school during lesson time, I saw a student in uniform arguing with a man. Some papers changed hands. As I approached, they both ran off and one of them dropped a wallet.

This item I am returning. In it you will find a large sum of money and the name of the owner. No doubt you will wish to investigate this incident.

Yours faithfully

S Lunn

You are the student concerned, and it is your wallet. The principal now requires an answer to the following questions in the form of a written statement:

- Why were you out of school during lessons?
- Who was the man?
- What were you talking about?
- What were the papers that changed hands?
- Why was there so much money in your wallet?

You should concentrate on accuracy and clarity.

Your statement should cover all five questions in detail.

Remember, this question tells you *what* to write and *how* to write it. So what can you learn straight away? Look at the information given in S Lunn's letter. This will help you decide what to include in your answer. You must concentrate on each fact supplied.

Have a quick practice at this. Make a mental note of four facts you have just learned from the situation in S Lunn's letter. Don't read on until you have done this.

Now check your list against ours. You should have the following:

- you know that S Lunn has witnessed a conversation or argument
- a school student and a man were involved
- some papers were exchanged
- money and a wallet were lost

To do the writing properly, you must pretend to be the student in the conversation/argument and write a statement for your principal. The word 'statement' should tell you exactly how to write the task. It could mean a letter to the principal or a report to him/her.

In directed writing, you *must* read the question carefully. It is much more of a test of reading than continuous writing is. You must not ignore any details and you must not change essential facts in the situation. Be careful though, as there is more reading to do. Look at the questions you are asked in the *five bullet points* provided. The question requires you to include answers to all five points. Leaving out any point will lead to losing marks.

Practice session

Practise the reading skill we have discussed so far in the following example.

One of your teachers is about to retire. She has taught in your school for many years and, therefore, you know her quite well. You have been asked to write a farewell letter to her on behalf of your class, thanking her and wishing her well in the future.

Use the following information:

- She has not been well lately
- She teaches English
- She is very strict, but always fair
- She is good at comforting depressed students
- She likes flowers, especially orchids
- She has taken your class on several school trips
- She is intending to travel to Europe soon

Your letter should be 200–300 words long and set out correctly.

Let's see what this one tells us about *what* to write and *how* to write it. When you have read it carefully, complete the following in the spaces provided:

❶ From the information given in the situation, list three facts which will be helpful in deciding *what* you include in your answer.

❷ Ask yourself what kind of writing is required.

Compare your list with the one that follows. If you have read this carefully, you will know that:

❶
- we must makc thc teacher a female
- she is retiring and therefore *not* just moving on to another job
- she is an experienced teacher

❷ The piece of writing required is a *letter* in which you must thank her and wish her well.

As long as you also know what is required in the bullet points, you will have a very good grasp of what material is needed in this task.

Golden rule

It is vital that you read the question carefully. Directed writing is not just a task of writing but of reading and understanding. Always remember that you are going to be directed towards *what* to do and *how* to do it.

3

How is directed writing like continuous writing?

With all this stress on reading, you must be wondering if directed writing is at all like continuous writing. Well, of course, it is. Directed writing, like continuous writing, also tests your writing skills, even though you have to use reading skills as well.

In the Cambridge syllabus for English language it states that candidates must, '... use language to inform and explain' *and* '... employ different forms of writing to suit a range of purposes'.

Both of these points are aimed particularly at directed writing. Much importance is put on your ability to write effectively; therefore everything you learned for continuous writing about:

- varying your sentence structure
- using a suitable vocabulary
- punctuating accurately and helpfully
- writing in paragraphs
- spelling correctly

will all be essential in directed writing as well.

Here is evidence of what we mean. Both of the following extracts are from actual exam scripts for the first question printed in the last chapter. Which do you think is the better piece of writing?

Piece 1

> On the morning of 11th November 1997, at about 10.00 a.m., I was meeting my father outside the school gate. Prior to this, I had sought and received the permission of my class tutor to be temporarily excused from class so that I could take some items from my father… We looked like we were arguing as my father was scolding me for being irresponsible and I was attempting to tell him that I had to return to class…

Piece 2

> I went out of school during the lesson because I want to meet my brother. In the class there were no teacher and I decided to went out of school. We're talking about a key. My brother ask me where I put the key house. So I told him where hide the key. The papers which we changed hands is a letter…

We hope you agree that Piece 1 is better than Piece 2. In fact, Piece 1 would receive a very high grade if it continued like this and Piece 2 would get a very low one. Writing skills are just as vital in directed writing as for continuous writing. Checking your work to get rid of any errors is very sensible too. Indeed, we would like to suggest that you should not write for the entire 30 minutes you are given for directed writing. Candidates who do write for the whole time tend to ignore their errors. Therefore, we suggest that you plan for five minutes at the beginning, then write for about 20 minutes. That will leave you about 5 minutes to check your work thoroughly. It really is worth the effort.

Golden rule

Apply the good writing habits learned for continuous writing to directed writing. Check your work to ensure that you have not made any mistakes.

How does directed writing differ from continuous writing?

Though directed writing and continuous writing are very similar, they do not test the same skills. For one thing, directed writing involves more skill in reading. What other differences should we be aware of?

For continuous writing, you choose your composition from a list of titles. In directed writing there is only one question for every exam. Therefore you must make sure you have been taught, and have revised, the types of functional writing that you are likely to be asked for in the exam:

- letters
- reports
- accounts
- statements
- magazine articles
- speeches

This section of the book will help you do just that.

Golden rule

Practise all the possible types of directed writing tasks you may encounter as you will not be able to choose an alternative during the examination.

5

Let's attempt an actual past exam paper

Let's look more closely at an actual exam paper and make an attempt at it. Let's look again at the question in Chapter 2.

Your principal received the following letter:

Dear Sir

As I was walking near your school during lesson time, I saw a student in uniform arguing with a man. Some papers changed hands. As I approached, they both ran off and one of them dropped a wallet.

This item I am returning. In it you will find a large sum of money and the name of the owner. No doubt you will wish to investigate this incident.

Yours faithfully

S Lunn

You are the student concerned, and it is your wallet. The principal now requires an answer to the following questions in the form of a written statement:

- Why were you out of school during lessons?
- Who was the man?
- What were you talking about?
- What were the papers that changed hands?
- Why was there so much money in your wallet?

You should concentrate on accuracy and clarity.

Your statement should cover all five questions in detail.

In Chapter 2, we said something about the situation in this question and worked out a lot about what we have to write and how we have to write it. Now let's concentrate on the other clues in the question.

Look at what it says: 'The principal requires... *a written statement*'. Furthermore, the principal would like you to write '... *with accuracy and clarity*'. Students often ask how closely the examiner will stick to these requirements. The answer is that (s)he will keep very closely to what it says because (s)he is guided by the question in the same way you are. So, you have to take these clues seriously. What should you learn from them?

❶ If you are asked to write a statement, it would be silly to turn this writing into anything else, such as a newspaper article. If it's supposed to be a statement, then it ought to be a statement; that means producing a report or possibly a letter.

❷ Certainly, if the principal wants a clear, accurate statement it is no good if you turn this into a creative piece of writing that you try to make as exciting as possible, even if it means distorting the truth. It isn't supposed to be an imaginative essay.

❸ Also, if the question asks for '... accuracy and clarity', you mustn't confuse the issue by introducing unclear or inaccurate details, for example, by saying it was 'cloudy or sunny' and thereby showing you are an unreliable witness. On the other hand, the exact time of day (such as 9.25 am) might be vital in verifying the story and allowing the principal to confirm it with the teacher concerned.

❹ The question states that *you* are the student concerned. Don't, therefore, make the mistake of reporting as if it is someone else. Yes, this sounds obvious but this is what some candidates do when they don't read the question carefully enough. It is precisely what one student really did in the exam, when he wrote, 'After that, I saw a man arguing with a student.'

This is clearly wrong and is the result of a hasty reading of the question. By the same token, you mustn't pretend to be S Lunn, or anyone else for that matter. You must be the student concerned and you must be prepared to answer the principal's questions in your letter or report.

❺ The question states that you should answer all five points *in detail*. This does not mean that you have to deal with them in equal detail. You can give more emphasis to some points than to others – but remember, you must cover them all. This would be true of any directed writing task.

Golden rule

Be clear and accurate both about what you write and how you write it. Answer all the questions and avoid contradictions, ambiguities and confusion.

Practice session

Now try to write this statement, keeping in mind the points we have discussed so far. Remember the time limit and the amount you must write. Obviously, we have only started revising this type of task so don't be intimidated by it – have a go at it and enjoy it!

Once you have written the piece you can compare what you have done with the following example of an actual exam script. This is one that we think deserves a very good mark indeed. At the moment we are not concerned with how this student begins and ends the letter – only with the quality of the writing in the body of the letter itself. It isn't supposed to be the perfect piece as yet (we still have some way to go) but it is a very useful one for setting us a high standard to aim at, at this stage.

On the morning of the 11th of November 1997, at about 10.00 am, I was meeting my father outside the school gate. Prior to this, I had sought and received the permission of my class tutor to be temporarily excused from class, so that I could take some items from my father, which were due to be given in on that day.

My father handed me my end of year examination result slip which he had signed so I could return it to the school, as well as the consent form for the Track and Field Training Camp which I will be taking part in. I had forgotten to bring these papers to school earlier that morning. We looked like we were arguing as my father was scolding me for being irresponsible, and I was attempting to tell him I had to return to class.

My father then quickly left for work as he was already late, and I rushed back to class. However, in my haste, I did not place my wallet in my pocket carefully and it dropped to the ground. The wallet contained one hundred dollars which my father had earlier given to me, to pay to the school bursar (this was the fee for the Track and Field Training Camp). I have since handed in my consent form and result slip to the relevant teachers.

Practice session

Now that you are into the swing of this type of work, you could have a go at the one about the teacher in Chapter 2 on page 80.

6 Assessment objectives

Here is another directed writing task from a recent exam paper.

You are cycling along a road near a sugar cane processing plant and, as you approach an intersection, you see a tourist's hired car collide with a large lorry from the factory.

The police want a clear picture of what happened.

- What was the position of each vehicle?
- How much damage had been done?
- Was anyone hurt?
- What was done to assist the people involved?
- From what you saw, who was to blame?
- Can you make any suggestions to prevent further accidents at this spot?

Write your eyewitness account of the incident, answering the above questions.

This is another occasion when the candidates are expected to write a report, an eyewitness account of what they saw, but for the police this time.

Here, you can apply the lessons you have learnt about reading the questions carefully. For example:

- it would be foolish to write as if the accident happened anywhere other than at an intersection
- the report would have to be written for the police and no one else
- it would be no use writing a report for the local newspaper (you would get some marks but not as many as if you did it properly)
- also, you would have to consider both vehicles, not just one

- finally, the accident would have to take place outside a sugar cane proccssing plant and no other type of plant

Apart from this, we must remember the other vital aspects:

- you should not submit a piece of creative writing, turning this into a dramatic piece of action
- you should make the report accurate and clear, with no confusion or ambiguities
- write about all six points in detail but not necessarily in equal detail

Fortunately, there is even more help at hand. Every year the principal examiner for the paper has to write a new marking scheme for directed writing because it contains a different situation each time. He or she provides assessment objectives which make it very clear which aspects of the exercise are the crucial ones. These assessment objectives help the examiners decide whether the test has been done properly. In this case the principal examiner wrote that this question was to test the candidate's ability to:

❶ Write a report on the accident that communicates information and opinion clearly, accurately and economically.

❷ Carry out the instructions as detailed on the question paper regarding the particular information required.

❸ Write in accurate standard English, using a style and tone appropriate to the task.

What further lessons can we learn from these assessment objectives? There are some very important words to take notice of. The first of these is 'economically'. At first, this may seem strange when the question also asks you to give some information in detail. However, that's the idea; certain points have to be covered in detail, and you only have about 300 words, so you must be economical overall.

It is therefore vital that you do not introduce any *unnecessary* detail. You should never introduce material just for the sake of it. For example, it would be a waste of time saying what the people in the crash are talking about or how tall they are or what they weigh. This doesn't help the police at all. On the other hand, the colour or make of the car might help to identify a dangerous driver, and/or a comment about the height of the surrounding vegetation might explain some of the hazards of the spot and account for the accident. Here are some examples of exam scripts.

First, we'll show you an example of someone introducing unnecessary detail:

Piece 1

A few minutes before, the tourist's car had overtaken us and it was travelling at great speed. We noticed it in particular because the child in the back was wearing a baseball cap like the one I had bought for my son the week before.

So far so good – the witness has been observant and the reason for noticing the car is a convincing one. Unfortunately, the candidate now makes the mistake of trying to add too much to this detail. He goes on...

Piece 2

At first my son had not appreciated the baseball cap I had bought for him because the colours reminded him of a football team that he did not like. Eventually we had persuaded him to keep it because the cap was that of a team which was top of the league and obviously very successful. We told him he would be the envy of all his friends.

Now this may well be interesting in other circumstances, but it certainly doesn't help here; it isn't going to help the police with their enquiries. The writer got carried away with irrelevant detail.

The next extract is much better, with some carefully selected and appropriate detail as an answer to the fourth bullet point of the original question – what was done to assist the people involved?

Piece 3

> Fortunately, a man who was passing in his car used his handphone to call for an ambulance. Meanwhile, I used a handkerchief to stop the blood on the woman's forehead and the driver of the lorry tried to wake up the unconscious man. Luckily, the ambulance from the nearby hospital arrived within minutes and, after giving the victims some help, the paramedics took the casualties away on stretchers.

This is much better, isn't it? That detail about the man with the cellular phone is just right – it is realistic and helps to convey the seriousness of the moment. Above all, it is economical – brief enough to add something without distracting the reader's attention. This sort of detail would create a very good impression in the examiner's mind.

Golden rule

Be very selective about extra details which you think might add interest. You must be sure that these details make the situation clearer and more accurate.

Another crucial expression in the assessment objectives is 'accurate standard English', and you will be familiar with this from the section on continuous writing. But are you quite as sure about the 'style and tone' being appropriate to the task? The correct style would mean writing formally or informally, depending on the situation, and in the correct format. Selecting the correct tone means having the ability to write in a voice that is suited to the situation you are in and the person to whom you are writing. For example, you should be friendly when talking to a relative, or respectful when addressing someone in authority. What tone of voice should be used when giving a report to the police on an accident? Should you, for example, be light-hearted if someone has been injured in the accident, or should you be serious? Obviously the latter would be more acceptable. It would also help to be respectful and concerned because then you are more likely to be taken seriously. If you are only bothered about what you were doing at the time, that would be far too self-centred for the purpose of this report and therefore would be the wrong tone.

Above all, you should sound as if you want to be helpful and it might be good at the end of the report to say you are willing to answer any other questions the police might have, even though there shouldn't be too many if you have been suitably clear and accurate in what you have written.

Practice session

> Here are two directed writing tasks which need to be written in completely different tones of voice. Try both of them, allowing yourself 30 minutes for each. Concentrate on the tone of voice and don't forget all that we said about being economical in your writing.

Exercise 1

You are in hospital recovering from an operation. Your parents are away. You need to buy some personal items. You also need various books and notes for examination revision. You have borrowed some things which must be returned urgently.

Write a letter to a school friend in which you explain what has happened; ask for help; give news about yourself and your family; ask for news of school and other friends; and add other details of interest to you both.

Make your letter friendly and informative.

Exercise 2

A local businessman has offered a piece of land, about the size of two football pitches, to the school for use by the pupils.

It is near the school and it has a large, old, single-storey building on it. Your principal has asked you to make suggestions for the use of the building and land. You are required to offer him a written statement covering the following points:

● What is the intended use?
● What improvements and repairs will be needed?
● What are the expected benefits to students and local residents?

Golden rule

Make sure you adopt a tone of voice suitable to the task. You will learn more about this in the following chapters.

7 How are reading and writing marks allocated?

Look at this past paper question:

A cyclone warning was broadcast at 0800 hours.

- Describe carefully where you live.
- What precautions did you and your family take?
- What were others doing?
- How much damage was done?
- To what extent were your precautions satisfactory?

Use all five points to write a letter to a friend overseas, giving an account of the event outlined above.

You must cover all five points in detail.

Allocation of marks

We have been saying all along that directed writing tests both writing and reading skills. When the principal examiner set this question, he had to decide how to allocate the marks so that he could reward both the writing and the reading skills of each candidate. In this particular case, he allocated 15 marks out of 20 for the language skills and the remaining 5 for the content or bullet points which reflect how well you have read and thought through the question.

Language (15) + Content (5) = 20

You may be surprised to see how uneven these marks are, but you must remember that this is still primarily a language exam, so that aspect gains more marks. This doesn't mean that content is unimportant — far from it. Remember that your content has to be good throughout (and not just in the bullet points) to enable you to show your language skills.

Here's another example, this time with more than five content or bullet points:

After a bus journey, you arrive at a relative's home to stay for a few days. You find that you have picked up the wrong bag.

Write an account of what happened, using the points below, and adding details of your own.

- How and when you discovered the mistake
- What was in the bag(s)
- What your feelings were
- Who else was involved
- How your stay was affected
- What finally happened

You should arrange and expand the above notes.

(NB The wording of this past paper question has been altered very slightly.)

Look at this example of an actual answer to the question above, with ticks put in the margin where the examiner found the answers to the bullet points.

Last year I learned a valuable lesson about myself but I had to go through a difficult time in order to achieve this. It all happened when my mother entrusted me with the job of delivering some important documents relating to a land deal to my cousin who lived in a town 70 kilometers from my own. I stupidly insisted on carrying the papers in an old (and, as I thought, unique) travelling bag rather than in something more substantial.

[✔2]

I caught the bus near the old post office in my town and travelled for a little over an hour. The journey seemed slow but pleasant enough as I idly chatted with several people. Passengers got on and off the bus at regular intervals. I was not at all alarmed until I reached my destination and I discovered to my dismay that the bag next to me was not my own, a realisation that dawned on me when I saw unfamiliar scratches on the side of it. Imagine my horror when I found that the bag I had contained nothing more valuable than some recently purchased fruit; I had to accept the fact that the young lady dressed in a striking blue suit who had been sitting near me earlier had unwittingly left the bus with my bag!

[✔1]

[✔3]

[✔4]

My overnight stay at my cousin's was not a happy one. Not only did I feel extremely foolish but also guilty that I had caused such anguish. My cousin hardly spoke to me after his initial explosion of anger and his normally happy household was never more subdued.

[✔5]

Luckily for me, the documents in my bag contained my cousin's name and address and the lady who had walked off with them proved to be very honest. She turned up at my cousin's house, full of apologies, and we exchanged the bags. Unfortunately, the worst was still to come as I had to face my mother and admit I had not taken my responsibility seriously enough!

[✔6]

All the points are there, properly dealt with and the candidate gains the full six content marks. As the script is also very good linguistically, it would gain a high mark for language as well.

Golden rule

Always think in terms of two sets of marks for your directed writing. Both content and language marks are vital.

8 Are the bullet points useful in any other way?

Bullet points provide a structure for your answer. The points are not necessarily separate paragraphs, but they can go a long way towards planning your response. Let's think about content/bullet points in this way. Look again at this question which we first saw in Chapter 6:

You are cycling along a road near a sugar cane processing plant and, as you approach an intersection, you see a tourist's hired car collide with a large lorry from the factory.

The police want a clear picture of what happened.

- What was the position of each vehicle?
- How much damage had been done?
- Was anyone hurt?
- What was done to assist the people involved?
- From what you saw, who was to blame?
- Can you make any suggestions to prevent further accidents at this spot?

Write your eyewitness account of the incident, answering the above questions.

With only 200–300 words to write, it would be reasonable to expect either three or four paragraphs (probably three), depending on the particular task. Your piece would be far too broken up if it had five or six paragraphs, even though there are six content points. Your job is to combine your material so that the three paragraphs contain the points in the most sensible arrangement.

Have a go at this. Arrange the material to fit the three paragraphs. Which content/bullet points would you put into each paragraph?

Here is the way it might be arranged:

- Para 1 – The position of the vehicles *and* the damage done
- Para 2 – The extent of the injuries, the assistance given *and* who was to blame
- Para 3 – Suggestions to prevent further accidents

To give you an idea of how well this can be managed in an exam, this is what one candidate wrote. As you read it, focus on the way it is paragraphed.

I was cycling behind a contract car in which there were two tourists, a man and a woman, when we came to an intersection. We were near a sugar cane factory and the car was negotiating the intersection when suddenly a lorry came from the opposite direction. When the drivers saw what was about to happen, both applied their brakes but it was too late and the two of them collided, sending both vehicles into a nearby field. The left side of the car was severely damaged (there were dents everywhere).

The woman who was in the passenger seat was injured. She had a broken arm; fortunately her husband only has some cuts and bruises from the broken windows. The lorry driver was not injured and his lorry was not badly damaged. With the help of some people who had gathered on the spot, we managed to get the tourists out of the car and rush them to the hospital. In my opinion the lorry was to blame as the driver was speeding and did not stop at the intersection.

The spot is a dangerous one as there have been similar accidents previously. I think that the installation of traffic lights would help to reduce this kind of accident in the future. If this eventually is not possible, a constable at the spot at peak hours and a few signs saying 'dangerous intersection' or 'beware of lorries' should prevent further accidents.

No one is saying that this is a perfect answer in every respect; for example, it should be a little longer to get slightly closer to the 300 words, and it could have a little more detail (you can read about this in later chapters). However, we are only looking at this as an example of paragraphing, and in this respect the answer is a very good one. It certainly demonstrates how well six points can be handled in three, well-ordered paragraphs. There would be nothing wrong with four paragraphs but any more than this would tend to make the writing too broken up.

Practice session

How would you arrange the following five bullet points into three paragraphs?

A cyclone warning was broadcast at 0800 hours.

- Describe carefully where you live.
- What precautions did you and your family take?
- What were others doing?
- How much damage was done?
- To what extent were your precautions satisfactory?

Use all five points to write a letter to a friend overseas, giving an account of the event outlined above.

You must cover all five points in detail.

Finally, let's go back to the example about the student who lost a wallet outside school (*see Chapter 2, page 78*). Notice how the following candidate has been sensible enough not to try and split the writing up into too many paragraphs when writing this report on the incident.

On the 25th October 1997, I met Mr. John Lim at the back gate of the school as, on that particular day of the week, I have a free period. Mr Lim happens to be an old friend of the family. He was due to have given some tickets to my father, however on the night of the 24th October, he called to say he was unable to pass them to him directly, but wondered if he could possibly hand them to me instead. My father agreed, and thus I became an errand boy for Mr. Lim.

Although the circumstances must appear to you to be most dubious and suspicious, the large sum of money was for Mr. Lim, since the tickets (the so-called 'papers' that changed hands) happen to be for the 1997 Heinekin Open Tennis ATP tour finals, and do not come cheaply. You see, my father and I are serious tennis fans. It will sound hilarious but the so called 'argument' Mr. Lunn happened to see was in fact the two of us engaging in a heated but friendly discussion about whether Michael Chang was better than Jonathan Stark or not.

I am terribly sorry that this misunderstanding occurred but I do believe that Mr. Lunn may have exaggerated the facts, since both Mr. Lim and myself did not, as he alleges, run away. I thank him for returning my wallet in its original state, and am exceptionally grateful that you've given me the opportunity to explain myself. Mr. Lim was also concerned when he realised I'd lost my wallet with the cash inside. He would be most delighted if you could call him at his office to clear up this most unfortunate misunderstanding. Thank you.

Again, this isn't faultless (you can probably see things you could improve upon) but three paragraphs are enough to convey the information. If you were able to include more detail, or if you felt that one bullet point needed a paragraph of its own, then four paragraphs would be perfectly acceptable.

Golden rule

You must use all the content/bullet points. They can be in any order as long as the order is sensible. Unless the circumstances are exceptional, three or four paragraphs should be sufficient.

Practice session

You can now extend your understanding of this aspect of your work by arranging the following past paper questions into sensible paragraphs, and then completing the writing of the answers within the time and word limits.

Exercise 1

When you and a friend were walking by the sea, you witnessed an accident.

Write an account of what happened, using the following points and adding further details where necessary:

- sudden change in weather
- collision
- serious damage
- bodies in water
- rescue attempts
- survivors brought ashore
- argument about blame

(NB The wording of this past paper question has been altered very slightly.)

Exercise 2

A rich, local businessman has offered a large sum of money to finance a student on a month's visit to another country. It will be granted to a student who is well-qualified, and who will benefit greatly from the experience.

Include the following ideas in your application:

- Your own special qualifications and interests
- Country chosen and why
- What you would like to do there (places, activities)
- What you would tell the people about your own country
- What you hope to gain from the visit

Using the above notes, and including other details if you wish, write your application.

9

Content/bullet points — how much do I write?

Now that you have learnt to put the content or bullet points into the order in which you are going to write about them, you must now think about how much to write about each one. Remember that you do not have to write the same amount for each content/bullet point.

Let's look at this example again to prove this point.

Your principal received the following letter:

Dear Sir

As I was walking near your school during lesson time, I saw a student in uniform arguing with a man. Some papers changed hands. As I approached, they both ran off and one of them dropped a wallet.

This item I am returning. In it you will find a large sum of money and the name of the owner. No doubt you will wish to investigate this incident.

Yours faithfully

S Lunn

You are the student concerned, and it is your wallet. The principal now requires an answer to the following questions in the form of a written statement:

- Why were you out of school during lessons?
- Who was the man?
- What were you talking about?
- What were the papers that changed hands?
- Why was there so much money in your wallet?

You should concentrate on accuracy and clarity.

Your statement should cover all five questions in detail.

It would obviously be difficult to write the same amount about the second bullet point as the third, so don't try. For some points you will gain the mark by saying relatively little, if there is little that can be said. However, do not be tempted to write very little for every content/bullet point, in the belief that as soon as you mention the point you will get the mark. Imagine a candidate simply writing in answer to the content/bullet points:

- I had gone to the toilet.
- The man was my brother.
- We were talking about a football match.
- The papers that changed hands were tickets.
- The money was to buy a ticket for my friend.

Strictly speaking, these are answers to the questions and all sensible enough. However, you would hardly say that such answers were trying very hard to impress the examiner. After all, the examiner does use some discretion when awarding the marks and, in the above example, he would be very reluctant to reward all five marks for content points.

As we have said, some points are quite difficult to add much information to and we have to accept just a small addition. For example, if you say, 'The man was my brother' it would be very easy to add a little extra without making it irrelevant – 'The man was my brother Paul, who is two years older than I am.' Even with this little addition the examiner would award the mark quite readily.

Let's consider the point about what the two people were saying to each other. You could just write, 'We were arguing about the time.' However, this is hardly a very full answer. It simply doesn't say enough to give the principal a clear, accurate idea of what was going on. Also, if you consider that the connection between the time and the money in the wallet is not obvious, it leaves the principal guessing about the truth. It leaves as much unexplained as it does explained.

So let's have another go. What about this?

> My father and I had started talking about the need for me to pay
> my school fees on that day. At first he spoke in a friendly manner
> but he became increasingly annoyed because I had left the money
> at home when I had left for school, a mistake which now caused
> him to be late for work. The tone of his criticism became more and
> more harsh as he generalised about the irresponsibility of young
> people.

Now this is much better. It seems a reasonable explanation of the
circumstances.

It's also possible someone could say that the one person was a
gangster, and that they were arguing about the supplying of drugs.
Quite frankly, though, we wouldn't advise this. It would begin to
sound a bit unlikely and more like an imaginative story, the sort of
writing best kept for continuous writing.

Practice session

> Now try making each content point long enough and also
> interesting. Let's begin with the point about, 'What were the
> papers that changed hands?'

It would be extremely simple to say:

- The papers that changed hands were not at all important.
- The papers that changed hands were for my teacher.
- The papers that changed hands were several letters.
- The 'papers' that changed hands was actually an envelope.

All of these answers are either:

- vague
- not sufficiently explanatory
- inaccurate

However, these were all answers given in a recent examination.

You can do better than this. Have a try. Write the whole answer, making sure you add something significant to each point.

Compare your answer with this one, which we think is very good.

I refer to the incident whereby I was seen outside the school during lesson time exchanging papers with a man. The incident occurred yesterday at around 9.30 am.

The Science teacher, Miss Wong, was in the middle of the lesson when we were interrupted by Miss Tan, my Maths teacher. She informed me that my father was outside the school waiting to see me urgently. He was unable to enter the school as there was no parking space in the compound and was afraid that his car, parked by the road, would be towed away. I quickly ran outside where my father informed me that I had accidentally taken his presentation notes for a particular meeting that morning; he told me to run back to class to get them for they were in my folder.

After returning with the materials, he handed me my Science project notes. Apparently I had mistaken the two for each other and brought the wrong ones to school. At this point, we were arguing quite ferociously as my father was in a rather foul mood. He felt annoyed at having to make his clients wait, while I insisted that the mix up was not my fault as I had been very tired the night before and was not feeling well when I packed my schoolbag.

> After the quarrel, my father saw a policeman approach his car, some ten metres away, and ran towards him to explain things. I turned back to class and unknowingly dropped my wallet. The wallet contained a hundred and thirty dollars, which was meant to pay for a series of textbooks which the school has ordered for us. I received the wallet this morning, with the money in order and untouched. Thank you for your attention.

This is cleverly handled. We learn that the man is her father and he has had trouble parking. Not only do we learn that she missed the science lesson but it is the maths teacher who has to come to get her; the heated conversation is the result of clients being frustrated; we don't just realise which papers are exchanged but we feel how rushed the early morning preparations have been; finally we learn about the amount of money and not only that it was for textbooks, but that the school had ordered them. This is an excellent case of adding just the right amount of extra information so that we feel the candidate wants to give us more than the minimum but hasn't made the mistake of overdoing it and losing the thrust of the explanation.

Here's another example:

> Write a report suitable for publication in a newspaper, based on the question below:
>
> **The hero's welcome**
>
> A close relative who risked his life to save a friend, returned home from abroad. You arranged a special welcome for this hero.
>
> - Where did he arrive?
> - How was he welcomed?
> - Who made the speeches and what was said?
> - What else was done to honour him?
> - How did he respond to the occasion?
>
> You must cover all five points in detail.

Again, it's difficult to write as much about the first three content points as about the last two, so don't try.

For all the points, the simple way is to say:

- He arrived at the airport.
- My family went to meet him.
- My father made a speech and said he was proud.
- The family took him for a meal to celebrate.
- He was very grateful for all the attention he was given.

This is too simple. It would be very easy to add extra information without making it irrelevant: 'He arrived late in the afternoon at Changi Airport in a jumbo jet belonging to Singapore Airlines.'

Practice session

Have a go at bullet points 2 to 5. When you are adding to the content/bullet points, don't write too much as you will soon go over your limit of 200–300 words. Besides, there are still more details to think about which we will tackle later on.

Golden rule

Think carefully about how much to write for the content points. Either too little or too much will be a disadvantage. Write enough to show you have not simply given the minimum, but don't write so much for each one that the explanation becomes too complicated.

10 How will the content/bullet points be assessed?

In this chapter you will see some more examples of directed writing answers in order to appreciate how the examiner decides whether or not to award the content/bullet point. The following are examples of the most common mistakes. Let's go back to our task about the cyclone warning.

A cyclone warning was broadcast at 0800 hours.

- Describe carefully where you live.
- What precautions did you and your family take?
- What were others doing?
- How much damage was done?
- To what extent were your precautions satisfactory?

Use all five points to write a letter to a friend overseas, giving an account of the event outlined above.

You must cover all five points in detail.

Example 1

Here the candidate is trying to answer bullet point number one and say carefully where they live. The candidate writes, 'I live in Mauritius, at Quatre Bornes.' Obviously this is correct and sensible enough, but it is far too short to convince the examiner that much effort has been made. What makes it particularly disappointing is that the candidate has been asked for a letter, so this information has been given in his address at the top of the page. Not only is the information brief, it repeats what has already been said! It would not be too difficult to say, for example, 'I live to the north of my town in a large house which is situated very close to a well-known local wet market.' This sentence isn't that much longer than the original, but it is far more adventurous.

111

Now your turn. What would you have written in response to the instruction, 'Describe carefully where you live'?

Example 2
It is possible to go to the other extreme and write far too much. Let's take the second point of the question about what precautions were taken before the cyclone. One candidate wrote,

> My whole family was involved in the precautions that had to be taken. My father made sure that pieces of wood were nailed onto the window frames to make sure that the glass was not smashed during the height of the storm. Mother went to the shops as quickly as she could and cooked several meals that would last us through that hazardous time. She cooked curried chicken, rice and peas, some loaves of bread and lots of the small cakes that my brothers and I like. To help out even further, my sister went to the store and bought as many candles as she was allowed to take.

This is actually quite good writing, but did we really need all that information about what the mother cooked? There would be no hesitation in awarding the point, but this candidate has used over 100 words! Consequently, the whole letter became rather unbalanced.

What would you have written?

Example 3
Sometimes students in examinations will write something that shows how nervous and hasty they can be when under pressure. In answer to the third point of the question above, 'What were the others doing?' one candidate said that his neighbours were planning their holiday! I know it is easy to be wise after the exam, but it would be difficult to imagine a more unlikely activity during a cyclone warning! In such circumstances, an examiner would have some difficulty in awarding the point because the answer doesn't suggest much thought has gone into it.

What would you have written in answer to the question, 'What were the others doing?'

Example 4
Another way in which candidates can sometimes spoil their work through haste is when they contradict themselves. Just imagine the panic that was going through the mind of a candidate who described a particularly violent and destructive cyclone, the worst in living memory, which caused no damage at all – or a candidate who talked about a great deal of damage all around, even to the house, and then said in content point five that the precautions had been a great success!

You can do better. What would you say in answer to bullet point four, 'How much damage was done?'

Let's finish this chapter with a look at an example of this answer done very well.

I hope that you and your family are well. It's quite different for us, as two days ago our country was violently shaken by a cyclone.

Unfortunately, the position of our house creates some problems in cases of cyclones. Indeed my house is situated some distance away from the foot of a small hill and the rainfall drains part of the soil down to the back of our house. Heaps of soil always accumulate in our back garden after cyclones. On Saturday morning, everyone rushed to take necessary precautions. My father, as usual, quickly climbed on top of the house and removed the aerial. My mother closed all the windows and took inside the house anything important left outside such as our pet bird in its cage.

Meanwhile, Mr. Jerry our neighbour was also busy removing his aerial and his son carried inside some flower pots that Mr. Jerry had purchased at great expense. In fact the road was full of people rushing to buy necessary things.

At night the cyclone passed over our country with full force. We remained awake, watching with consternation for hours until the cyclone disappeared as quickly as it had arrived. There was obviously damage: not many trees had been left unscathed; scattered branches and broken flowers were strewn everywhere and of course the back garden was full of soil. Nevertheless, I'm glad to say that there was virtually no structural damage to our dwelling so I suppose it was worth the effort we put into our precautionary measures — certainly our bird was glad to have been indoors! Please write and tell me what has been happening to you.

Obviously it is always possible to criticise small points such as the repetition of the word 'house' in the second paragraph but, considering this was done under exam conditions by a 16-year-old (something examiners are very aware of), it is a very worthy effort and would gain a high mark. The examiner has five content marks at his/her disposal and would have no hesitation in awarding all five – the letter is the right length, the points are addressed sensibly and they are completed in a balanced, thoughtful way.

Should I add other details besides those for the content/bullet points?

Quite simply, the answer is yes, you should definitely include other material on top of what you have done already for the content/bullet points. The examiner likes to have proof that the candidate is prepared to put in extra effort, that the candidate is prepared to work to gain marks. Think of it in terms of this formula: a good answer will be a suitable mixture of the content/bullet points, some additional material to make the content points interesting or convincing, and further elaboration (which is what this chapter is about). Elaboration is the art of adding just the right amount of information that you haven't been asked for specifically. To revise this particular skill, we'll move on to other examples of directed writing.

You observe a person standing at a busy street corner offering handmade articles for sale.

Many people stop to look; few buy.

- What is being sold?
- How is the seller encouraging people to buy?
- What kinds of people are spending money?
- Why are sales infrequent?
- How could the seller have more success?

Write an article for your school magazine or local newspaper on the activity described above.

Use continuous English and appropriate style, making sure that you answer all five questions.

Let's start by using this example to summarise, in convenient steps, all we have done so far:

- The situation tells us that the person is on a street corner – nowhere else will do. The articles are handmade; we mustn't make them mass-produced. Not much is being sold. None of these facts must be altered.

- The next consideration is the bullet points, or content marks. All five must be answered, although not necessarily in equal detail. For example, it would be very difficult to write as much for the first point as for the last, without resorting to a boring list of articles.

- After considering the bare facts of the bullet points we must add a little to each to make them interesting, without introducing unnecessary detail. You should not just name the articles being sold, but say what colour they are, what they are made of or how much they cost. You certainly shouldn't talk about anything irrelevant, such as the price of similar articles you saw on a recent holiday.

- You could then think about the order in which you would deal with these points (they don't have to be in the order in which they are printed). Follow this up by deciding on the number of paragraphs (three or four) and which points will be dealt with in each paragraph.

- Next, take note of the fact that the question is asking for a magazine or newspaper article – no other piece of writing will do. You may think this obvious, but many candidates who took this exam actually wrote a letter to the newspaper. They ignored one crucial skill of directed writing – they did not read the question carefully.

- Think also about the tone appropriate to such an article. It's a fairly serious topic, isn't it? The seller isn't having the happiest of times. In fact his/her livelihood is at stake. Your approach should therefore be in keeping with this – probably sympathetic and certainly helpful. You wouldn't want to make it an attack on street sellers in general, as some candidates did in the exam.

Now we come to the whole point of this chapter. Once you have done all of the above, you are likely to have written close to 300 words, but not enough to consider that the job has been done. You therefore need to introduce some interesting and relevant elaboration, not directly of the content points this time but something that will bind all your answers to the bullet points. For example, you could start by briefly introducing the article with details of how you came across this seller and where (s)he was situated. Name the street corner and describe it – not just a description for the sake of it but something that captures the suitability or otherwise of the street corner as a location for selling the articles. It will introduce vivid local colour into your work. Examiners will appreciate this. Details of the seller's appearance will bring the person to life. Somewhere in your article you could mention how typical this seller was in local terms. Did (s)he stand out as being unusual, or was he just an average street seller who you might see all the time? In these ways you will successfully build a more interesting picture than by sticking strictly to the bare content/ bullet points. Don't forget, though, these extra bits must be relevant.

> **Practice session**
>
> With all of the above points in mind now attempt this question .

The following answer, taken from the exam, is quite a good one, not altogether deserving top marks, but very close. Incidentally, we've underlined the elaboration introduced by this candidate.

The 44th Street in town is a busy one and it is dotted with shops and stalls selling various interesting items of all sorts. Recently, at a busy street corner, a rather grubby-looking person has set up a small stall selling hand-made articles. His products are arranged on an old and rusty table but his woodcraft is quite beautiful, with items such as dolls, earrings, cups, toys and decorative objects which look strangely out of place in such modern surroundings.

From his appearance, I think he is just a beginner in his money-making business. He advertises his products by just putting up a dull-looking sign showing 'Woodcrafts' and he just stands there using his filthy hands to gesture at his products. Most of his potential customers are children and people who appreciate his art but his sales, as far as I can see, are infrequent and slumping. This has largely to do with his appearance and the way he treats his customers. On certain occasions, local inhabitants rebuke him when he is especially unpleasant to foreign tourists.

I approached him once and he smells of cigarettes and cheap scotch. He is not properly dressed and his clothing is shabby with patches of cloth here and there. He speaks to customers quite sharply and does not smile often. His pricing also has an impact on his sales. He sells a wooden doll for 20 dollars and that is far too expensive when its size is taken into consideration. In my personal opinion, his sales could be much better if he could dress properly and quit his smoking habit while he is working. Smiling might also help his profits. In order to increase these even further, he should hand out advertising slips to passers-by. He should also cut his prices and speak in a friendlier tone.   (304 words)

The underlined sentences are good indications of the sort of extra material that can give proper substance to the writing. They also serve another very important purpose. Each examiner will have several hundred scripts to mark, with the bullet points being the same for everyone. This, of course, produces a considerable degree of similarity in the answers. Obviously, no examiner is going to blame any candidate for this similarity, but it is always a pleasure to see fresh, original material which reveals the individuality of each candidate. For this reason, you should always try to introduce that little bit extra.

Golden rule

Think positively about elaboration. Don't feel you have to write too much, but look upon it as a chance to give your work an individual flavour.

What type of writing will be asked for in directed writing tasks?

Having to write an account is one of the most common directed writing tasks. Look, for example, at this past paper question:

Your school asked for volunteers to entertain, for a day, a small group of young people from another country. You were one of those chosen.

Write an account of what you did, considering some or all of the following points:

- Tour of the school
- Surrounding area
- Local activities
- Meeting friends and family
- Food

Did your guests enjoy themselves?

Let's approach this by considering the steps we have taken so far. These steps will increasingly become a routine way of approaching each task until it is second nature for you.

Step 1 – Check the essential facts of the situation
Look at the situation in this question and see what facts should be remembered – this will be a test of your reading. You must be a volunteer (therefore you are doing this willingly), the job you are doing must occupy a set period of time (a whole day), and the children you are in charge of are foreign. Furthermore, you are one of a group of people doing this job; therefore you have help. These are all essential facts which must not be forgotten. You are also required to say whether the group enjoyed itself.

Step 2 – Examine the content/bullet points
Look at the bullet points and see what else is essential. First of all,
take note of the fact that you are invited to use some or all of the
bullet points. In a case like this, it is just as well to use all of them
to cover the topic as fully as possible. This is particularly true
because there are only five points anyway, and you would expect to
need at least this many. You therefore have to note that a tour of
the school and surrounding area is required before you go to meet
your family. What surroundings are meant? Well, at least a look at
the sporting facilities at your school and/or the grounds, the play
area, perhaps even the busy town or quieter rural setting will be
expected. The mention of local activities in the bullet points would
suggest we are moving away from the school and through the local
neighbourhood before meeting up with your family/friends and
having something to eat. This already gives you plenty to think
about.

Step 3 – Add details for interest
Each of the bullet points will need some extra information to give
interest. For example, you could make a point of showing your
group your classroom, or introduce the group to a favourite teacher.
Talk of the sporting facilities could allow you to mention (not
describe) a game in which you were the star player. The local
activities would give you the chance to say something about a
shopping centre or local food market which you like to frequent.
Meeting your family will provide useful opportunities to indulge in
just a little description of a family member, while the food you have
will allow you to name your family's favourite dish. Above all else,
don't forget that you mustn't indulge in too much detail here.

Step 4 – Elaborate a little
Now think about elaborating so that the examiner knows you are
prepared to do that little bit more than the minimum. You can
mention where the children are from, how old they are, how many
boys and how many girls are in the group, or their reaction to the
new things you were showing them. More than anything, because
they are foreign, there will be opportunities to make comparisons

between your lifestyle and theirs. Lots of chances exist to introduce those individual details that will keep your writing fresh and different.

Step 5 – Plan your paragraphing
Three paragraphs would be just right:

- Para 1 – meeting the students, plus the tour of the school and surrounding area
- Para 2 – local activities
- Para 3 – meeting friends and family/having a meal

Step 6 – Consider the type of writing required
Time now to think about what kind of writing is required. If you came across the word 'account' in a continuous writing title you would be thinking of it as a story or narrative. This is not the case in directed writing. Here, the word 'account' is much closer to a report, a much more factual, informative piece of writing. No other piece of writing will do, not a newspaper article or even a letter. It must be a report-type account – and that leads us to your next decision.

Step 7 – Adopt an appropriate tone and style
What tone and style should you adopt? Now, this is quite a difficult question because normally the task will tell us the person to whom we are writing. If we knew it was our headmaster or our parent, it would be instantly obvious how we should address that person. Here, the question leaves us to make an assumption about who will receive our account. It's important not to panic just because no recipient is specified. Simply imagine a likely recipient and write the account in an appropriate tone and style. To our mind, the most likely recipient is a headmaster and therefore a polite, respectful, formal style and tone would be vital. On the other hand, it seems just as likely that a teacher has asked for the information, in which case, the tone would be similar.

An interesting approach might be to write a diary entry for yourself so that the tone would be much more familiar and conversational (but not careless). The point we are making is this: if the examiner makes clear who is to receive the account, then you must take note of this and write accordingly. However, if the account isn't aimed at anyone in particular, then you must decide and the examiner will be very happy to see what you decide, as long as it isn't absurd. Be aware of the fact that your work must have some indication of who is to receive the writing. If it is for your headteacher, then simply begin with the heading:

'For the attention of Mrs...'

and then write your account. If it is a diary entry, just start with the date.

Golden rule

Be prepared to think in terms of the steps we have outlined in this chapter. They will certainly give you confidence when it comes to planning your answer.

Practice session

The next few chapters will show you more of the different types of writing you may be asked for. Before you get on to those, though, there is another account on the next page you can practise writing.

One day you see two strangers near your school building. Later you discover that things have been stolen.

Write an account of the incident, using the following points and adding further details.

- Description of the strangers
- Where and when you saw them
- What they were doing
- Damage done
- Police informed
- Crime solved

(NB The wording of this past paper question has been altered very slightly.)

13 Writing letters

Writing a letter has always been an extremely popular choice among examiners. It is, after all, a basic form of communication, and there is a good chance that it will appear on exam papers very regularly. Of course, you never know what type of letter will be required. It is therefore only sensible to ensure that you feel confident when handling letters of all sorts.

Here is a fairly typical example from a past paper:

A local newspaper has published details of plans to construct a new hotel with tourist facilities and has asked for comments from its readers. Write your views in a letter to the editor.

You should consider:

- The effect on local people and the environment
- The choice of site for the building
- Job opportunities
- Expense
- Other possible uses for the land

You should begin
'Dear Sir,'

Remember to end with 'Yours faithfully,' and to add your signature.

This is the most formal of the letter types (one that starts 'Dear Sir,') and is sometimes referred to as a business letter, for obvious reasons. We will approach this question in the same systematic way we have approached previous ones.

Step 1 – Check the essential facts of the situation
Note the essential facts that you must not change nor omit:

- it's a new hotel
- it is to cater to tourists
- the plans have appeared in the local newspaper
- you are asked for your own views

Step 2 – Examine the content/bullet points
The bullet points demand:

- comments about people and the environment
- comments about the suitability of the site
- your views on the effect on jobs
- mention of what it will all cost – is it worth it or not?
- suggestions as to how the land might be used if you don't want the hotel

Step 3 – Add details for interest
Let's add a little extra to the bullet points. For example, when talking about the effect on people and the environment, you might add that a relative of yours will suffer because the hotel will block her view of the sea from her nearby house. On the other hand, mention of the effect on jobs could include the case of your cousin, who wishes to work as a chef in the hotel and wants the scheme to go ahead. What is helpful about both these suggestions is that they add a personal touch.

Step 4 – Elaborate a little
When it comes to elaborating on the points, some judgement is called for. This question seems to be the sort that requires quite a fair bit of writing just for the bullet points. Only a little elaboration will therefore be necessary – perhaps something about what else the money might have been spent on rather than a hotel, or perhaps some memory you have of the proposed site.

Step 5 – Plan your paragraphs

Arrange the material into paragraphs. Clearly, the first paragraph must indicate to the editor the reason for your writing. After that, you will only have room in that first paragraph to talk about the choice of site for the building, which seems to be the sensible place to start. The second paragraph can include most of the points, those concerning the effect on people and the environment, job opportunities and expense. Don't forget that if your work becomes quite detailed, this paragraph can be split into two. The final paragraph will address the issue of other uses for the land, and will then thank the editor for taking time to read the letter and printing it.

Step 6 – Consider the type of writing required

The type of writing required is a formal letter. There are two reliable ways of setting out a formal business letter. Stick to either of these and try not to complicate matters with variations. First of all, there is the traditional approach, as in this example:

West Secondary School,
27, West Coast Road,
Singapore 127314.
15th September, 1998.

The Editor,
The Straits Times,
Singapore.

Dear Sir,

Yours faithfully,

If you don't like that one, here is a more modern approach:

West Secondary School
27 West Coast Road
Singapore 127314
15th September 1998

The Editor
The Straits Times
Singapore

Dear Sir

Yours faithfully

The first example has punctuation, and the second doesn't. There are two vital points you need to remember. First, just because the two examples above are given, it doesn't mean that all other variations are wrong, but sticking to one of the above will prevent mistakes. The worst thing you can do is to mix the two styles. The second point to keep in mind is that, as with this question, if you are told to begin with the words 'Dear Sir', then you don't need to include the addresses at all.

Step 7 – Adopt an appropriate tone and style

Finally, what style and tone should you adopt? That decision will be based partly on your reaction to the building of the hotel. You can either be enthusiastic about the project and see the hotel as completely beneficial, or you can be entirely against the scheme and consider it detrimental. Equally valid would be to see both sides of the argument. There is nothing wrong with being partly in favour and partly against, as long as you don't say anything contradictory. Once you've decided on your standpoint, you must remember the other aspect of the tone. You are writing to a newspaper and therefore trying to persuade an editor to print your letter. For that reason you must be polite in your approach while being firm in your views. It's a tricky balance but one to which you must be sensitive.

You should now be in a position to have a go at this letter yourself. Before you do, have a look at one of the letters that was actually written for the exam by a candidate. The examples you have had so far in this directed writing section have usually been very good attempts, and most students would be extremely glad to have done so well. This one is a very average effort indeed, and we think it would be a good idea to think about it before you write yours to see what you can learn. Which parts of this letter do you think are good, and which not so good? What do you think of the tone, the paragraphing, the elaboration and so on?

Dear Sir,

I am writing to express my views on the construction of a new hotel at Cap Malheureux. According to the article published in your newspaper, it seems to me that the hotel has all the tourist facilities. I think that the construction of the hotel will be a boon for people living at Cap Malheureux.

I think that the organisers of this project have well chosen the site for the construction of the building. In this a region of the island there is a sandy beach and the blue sea is always calm there. It is also fortunate to note that the sea near Cap Malheureux is not polluted.

The hotel is also going to be constructed near the coastal village of Cap Malheureux. So people living in this area will be able to find a job in the hotel. Furthermore, Cap Malheureux has always been reputed for being a fishing village. So fishermen can sell their seafood to the hotel. Indeed the construction of the hotel will provide job opportunities to villagers and this will alleviate the problem of unemployment in this region. From what I have heard the cost of the venture is a very reasonable one, especially as it can only bring prosperity to the island.

I would be grateful if you would print my letter in full in your newspaper.

Yours faithfully,

Think carefully about the content here. Are all the points covered adequately? Is the vocabulary good or limited? Does the letter suffer from repetition?

Practice session

Now attempt your own letter. Try to do it within 30 minutes.

Of course, formal letters aren't the only ones likely to come up in the exam. Even more likely is the less formal letter, the sort that would be sent to a member of your family or a close friend. Look at this one:

> You are on holiday with friends in another area and are due to return home in four days' time. Unfortunately, you have had an accident which will prevent you from travelling for at least a fortnight.
>
> Write a letter to your parents, dealing with the following points:
>
> - How and where the accident happened
> - The treatment required
> - How you and your friends feel about the situation
> - What you need for the extra stay
> - When and how you will return home
>
> You may add any other information or requests, as necessary.

Let's stick to our method for answering this.

Step 1
Essential information that mustn't be forgotten:

- you are not alone but with a group of friends
- you are some way from home
- you should be travelling home
- you have been involved in an accident and cannot travel

Step 2
The bullet points insist that we mention:

- both how and where the accident happened
- how your physical injuries were treated
- how you are all coping emotionally
- money and provisions you might need
- your date of return

Step 3
Extra little touches to the bullet points might include:

- where you received treatment
- how long the treatment took
- where you are staying for the extra time, if it is different from before

Step 4
Elaborate on one or two points:

- what the holiday had been like until the accident
- what various people had done to help you in your difficulties

Step 5
Sensible paragraphing comes next:

- Para 1 – a greeting to your parents and the first content/bullet point about how and where the accident happened
- Para 2 – the main section containing content/bullet points two to four
- Para 3 – the final paragraph about your return home and possibly a word of comfort to your parents about the minor nature of your injuries, together with an assurance that you are looking forward to seeing them

If you wanted to, you could make this into four paragraphs depending on how much elaboration you can include. But don't split it up any more than this or it will be too fragmented.

Step 6

The type of writing required is the next consideration. This time a
friendly letter is required, set out as below:

```
                                              14, East Street,
                                              Kingston,
                                              Jamaica.
                                              8th May, 1998.


Dear Mum and Dad,




                        Your loving son,
                             John
```

Signing off when writing a friendly letter is often quite tricky
because you haven't got a standard phrase like 'Yours faithfully'. You
could say 'Yours sincerely' if you can't think of anything more
original, but we think it's often better to use an ending which is
appropriate to the person receiving the letter, for example, 'Your
loving daughter', 'Your loving nephew' and so on.

Step 7

The tone for this letter should be quite clear. It's known as a
friendly letter, and that's exactly what it must be. Writing very much
as you would speak to your parents would be ideal for this answer:
colloquial language, the occasional endearment, etc. This doesn't
mean being disrespectful; it simply means sounding as if you are
close to someone.

One fault that really spoils a letter for any examiner is when
candidates include overused phrases, for example, a first paragraph
which begins 'I am writing to…'. Just as important is to avoid sloppy
and obvious endings like 'I'm going to finish my letter now' or 'I'll
pen off now'. When the letter clearly finishes after saying this, you
can see what a terrible waste of words it is.

Golden rule

Learn the appropriate letter formats and concentrate
particularly on suitable openings and endings to the letters.

Write this letter now for practice.

Practice session

Here's another question to try. Remember to be especially careful
about the format, style and tone.

Write, using standard English, a letter to an elderly relative who
resides abroad, describing a picnic you enjoyed on a recent visit to
the interior of the island where you live.

Use the notes below, adding your own ideas to make interesting
reading.

- Journey by car to high plateau
- Site found/food prepared
- Sudden appearance of wild animal
- Reactions of various people
- Weather change
- Homeward bound

14 Writing a magazine article

The chance to write a magazine article is one that appeals to many candidates. Though it is not as common a question as a letter or an account, it is always a possibility. Don't worry about never knowing in advance what directed writing task you will be given – it will always be a situation within the grasp or experience of the average student. Take a look at this question:

> A popular teacher is leaving. You are asked to write a short article for your school magazine describing his or her services to the school. Using the ideas listed below, and adding material of your own, write your article:
>
> - How long at school
> - Subject(s) taught/pupils' examination successes
> - Activities outside the classroom
> - Kind/strict
> - His or her plans for the future.
>
> You may like to begin:
>
> We are very sad to be losing…

You should be accustomed to the following routine by now.

Step 1
Essential, unchangeable information: the teacher is a popular one, not one you dislike; you are describing what the teacher has done for the school.

Step 2
The content points are obvious: the length of service at school; his or her subject(s) and how successful s(he) was as a teacher; what s(he) did for extra-curricular activities;

something about his or her personality and finally what s(he) intends to do after leaving. Even when the points are as straightforward as this, it's well worth reading them again and rewording them in your mind to be clear about exactly what is expected.

Step 3
Little additions to the bullet points might be: mention of a trip s(he) had taken your class on for extra-curricular activities; a particular kindness or strictness s(he) had shown towards you, and so on.

Step 4
Elaboration will be needed. It may be an incident the teacher is famous for amongst his or her students – and why not make it a funny incident? So much of our writing has to be serious that a humorous event is a very welcome break. You could also write about a favourite lesson, or about the teacher's special way of teaching.

Step 5
Order your ideas in paragraphs:

- Para 1 – your sadness at his or her leaving and how long the teacher has been at the school, with a little additional information about where s(he) had taught previously
- Para 2 – subject(s)/exam success/activities outside the classroom
- Para 3 – his or her kindness/strictness/personality/and his or her plans for the future
- Para 4 – probably just a final short paragraph wishing the teacher every happiness in the future

Step 6
Now a word about the style of writing here. This is a magazine article, but the same would apply to a newspaper article if you were ever asked to write one. You don't have to copy the layout of a magazine by writing in columns. Far more important is to try and capture the essential style of a magazine article. The first and probably most important way of giving an immediate impression is to make up an interesting headline. You'll notice that the

instructions say you may begin your article in the way they suggest, but we think this is a good occasion to ignore the suggestion and go for an authentic sounding headline.

Step 7

The article should not sound too stiff and formal. Obviously it has to be respectful, but if it is too formal it will not have the warmth you would like to create in a piece about a favourite person. Make it grammatically correct, but also conversational, humorous and, above all, sincere.

Because it is an English exam you will understandably be keen to impress the examiner with your word power. There will be occasions here when impressive words will help. You can imagine the teacher being described as 'perceptive', 'imaginative' or an impressive 'linguist' and this level of language would be fine. However, if you overdo this sort of language it just sounds as if you are trying to show off, when really your article is attempting to praise someone else. The key here, as always with directed writing, is to make your writing appropriate to the occasion. If the article is for a school magazine, then remember that your main audience will be your fellow students, so again your language shouldn't be too inflated. Don't worry that you are not doing yourself justice; the examiner will be looking out for an appropriate tone, not necessarily just vocabulary.

Practice session

Try writing this article, applying the steps you have learnt.

Writing a speech

This sort of question sounds difficult, but by following the step by step approach you will be able to master it. Here's the question we will tackle:

An election is to be held in your school for members of the student council, a group set up to advise the principal on matters concerning student welfare and discipline. One of your friends hopes to be elected. You are preparing a speech in support of your friend.

You have the following notes to help you:

- Excellent games player
- Top in examinations
- Active in school clubs
- Organised end-of-year party
- Public speaking competition winner
- Always helps new students

Write out your speech in full, using the above list and other ideas of your own. You should write 200–300 words.

Let's prepare ourselves in the normal way.

Step 1
Essential, unchangeable information: the election is to the student council; welfare and discipline are vital issues; it is your friend you are supporting.

Step 2
Content/bullet points demand the following: you have to refer to sporting prowess and academic excellence; the social side of your friend makes him/her someone who has joined clubs and is obviously an organiser; the friend is definitely articulate, and finally you have to say something about his/her generosity and caring attitude towards new students.

Step 3

Additions to the bullet points might be: mention of his/her best sports and some details about a particularly inspiring feat of leadership; a short reminiscence about the end-of-term party (make it something relevant to the post he/she is going for, perhaps something to do with powers of organisation or administration).

Step 4

Elaboration can come in the form of details of other characteristics of your friend which will be helpful as a member of the student council – perhaps perseverance; certainly a good disciplinary record would be worth noting, considering this is what the principal wants advice about.

Step 5

With the six content/bullet points, paragraphing is straightforward: two points per paragraph for three paragraphs is ideal, and in the order in which they occur in the question.

Step 6

Now a special word about the style. This being a speech, you will have to think a lot more about how you would say this and not just how you would write it. Remember, it is not supposed to be primarily a written composition about your friend, but an address you are going to give to a mixed audience of teachers and pupils. This has an important implication. You must use all the skills that a public speaker would employ. You should use more short sentences than you might in a narrative or report. You should include a number of techniques such as asking questions of your audience, something like, 'Do you know of anyone more suited to the role?' This would involve your audience far more, which is what a speaker must do.

You could even break the rules slightly, for example by using the word 'and' at the beginning of a sentence, as in this opening to a paragraph – 'And as for his public speaking, he is second to none...'. Don't overdo it; just include enough to make it clear to the examiner that you know what kind of writing this is.

Finally, you wouldn't have to set out the speech in any complicated way, but it would be sensible to use speech marks at the start and the end of the speech to make it more realistic and it would be sensible to start in an appropriate way – 'Teachers and fellow students…'.

Step 7
The tone of the speech is as important as the style. Think about what you are trying to achieve. You are supporting someone, so be persuasive. Don't worry about showing too much bias in favour of one candidate, because that is what you are supposed to do. Be forceful in your attitude without being disrespectful towards the other candidates. Above all, there is nothing better to get an audience on your side than some humour – not too much or you will trivialise your friend's qualities. Perhaps you could recall a funny incident from the party your friend organised, but only if it shows him/her in a good light.

With all this in mind, now try to craft your speech.

Unit 2 — Further practice

In the section on directed writing you were encouraged to think of your work being planned in seven stages:

- a consideration of the situation in which you were placed
- the requirements of the bullet/content points
- extra material for the bullet/content points
- elaboration
- paragraphing
- the kind of writing required
- an appropriate tone and style

This section will allow you more practice at what we learned in the earlier chapters. We don't intend to repeat everything that has been said already. However, before you work on the examples below, it is worth pausing for a moment to reinforce two of the seven stages – the two that will make your work stand out as fresh, original and more thoughtful. We are talking about Step 3 (extra material for the bullet/content points) and Step 4 (the elaboration of ideas that you introduce into your writing).

Look at the following past paper question:

You are away from home visiting a relative. You have decided to write a letter to a friend.

You should:

- briefly describe where you are
- say why you are there
- mention something pleasant or unpleasant that has happened so far
- outline your plans for the next day
- explain the arrangements for your journey home

Write the letter to your friend. Use continuous English and appropriate style, making sure that you cover all five points.

Step 3 of our planning tells you that you should say more than the minimum for the bullet/content points. Therefore, for the first such point in the above question, it would be silly just to say that you were 'staying at my uncle's house' or 'in the country' or 'in France'. The last answer would be particularly pointless, as you would already have indicated this at the top of your letter and so you couldn't expect that to gain you the mark.

Step 4 of our plan suggests that you should elaborate to show the examiner that you are prepared to earn the marks. You should therefore be looking for opportunities to say more than is asked for with the bullet points. In this letter you can be asking about the family of your friend, if they are in good health, and what they have been doing. Remember, just enough to create the right impression, not so much that you go off the point and waste precious time.

Here are two examples of how this question was answered in the actual exam to give you an idea of where you stand. The first piece is a poor attempt. It is difficult to talk about exam grades for individual questions in isolation, but this letter would have difficulty in getting higher than a Grade U. It is printed here as it was written but without place names, and the top and bottom of the letter have been omitted.

Piece 1

Dear Eddy,

I have the great pleasure to write you this letter because you could not imagine how I miss you.

I am in ***********, I am in a great hotel named *************, I think that you know the hotel. The environment here is very pleasant, the people nearby are cool and respectful. They welcome straingers in a different and original way compared to us.

I am there to visit an grandmother because you know that I am now the responsible of the social security in ******************, and as **************** and ********************* are very linked, I was obliged to go and visit her all three months. So that I can see if there are help and assistance to give her.

Yesterday while I was visiting her, a little boy who had never spoken to his responsible party came up to me and said 'dady, dady, you are there an I will not be bad or sad.' My grandmother told me that she had gave him a photography and mine and since that day he consider me as his dady.

As I finish my visit I would like to return to ************* but for tomorrow I must take my grandmother to the seaside.

It is easy enough to see the faults in this effort. The sense is blurred, even obscured, there are many spelling and grammatical errors, and the last bullet/content point isn't even attempted. To be fair, there is some attempt to say more than the minimum in three of the four bullet points answered, but there is virtually no attempt to elaborate in any way, other than to say that the friend is missed.

Now see what can be done by a more competent student, one who might get a mark in the B range.

Piece 2

Dear Sanjay,

I am writing this letter to inform you that I am away from home visiting a relative. He lives at ***************. It is a coastal village situated at about eight kilometres from **********. It is very beautiful and peaceful here. There are about five hundred inhabitants and everyone knows each other. They are all very kind people.

I am here because the son is getting married soon and they invited me one week earlier. He is very excited of getting married and I understand him as I myself have recently met someone here. He doesn't live in *************** but comes to work in a sugar cane factory which is not so far away from my cousin's house. His name is ********** and I like him very much. I have met him when I have gone for a walk and he was going home after work. He is a cheerful and gregarious man. Furthermore, he has asked me to go out with him.

And next day I am planning to go the seaside with him. But there will not be just the two of us, my cousin and his fiance too will be coming along. Afterwards we have decided to go to ***************. There is a famous nightclub there and I think we will spend the night there. Isn't it exciting? Unfortunately the wedding is very soon and I must return home because of the work. I've told my boss that I will be away for only one week. Anyway, I don't regret at all that I have come here and perhaps one day we will be able to spend our holidays here.

Again we cannot ignore the weaknesses in this effort (it isn't a Grade A script) and the last bullet point is not earned. However, there is a welcome attempt to make something out of the question. All of the bullet points addressed have detailed additions to interest the reader. Furthermore, there are genuine attempts to elaborate by talking about the friendliness of the local inhabitants, giving informative descriptions of the boyfriend, and mentioning the visit to the nightclub, as well as the hope of spending future holidays in the same location. This is a pretty good effort, without being exceptional. We hope that both of these essays together give you a good idea of just what and how much to add. Remember you have a time limit for this question, as with all the others.

Now have a go at the following questions until you are really an expert at answering the directed writing section. All these examples are past paper questions or based on past paper questions. Remember to work through all the stages in order. Good luck!

Exercise 1

A relative of yours has been away for a long time and is now returning. You intend to hold a party to celebrate.

Write an account of the preparations you will make and of the party itself, using all of the points suggested below and adding ideas of your own:

- when you will hold the party
- invitations
- food and drink
- speeches
- activities

Exercise 2

You were visiting a friend in hospital when a fire broke out.

Write an account of what happened, using the points below and adding further details to create interest:

- how the alarm was given
- arrival of police and fire-fighters
- rescue incidents
- your escape
- skill and courage

Exercise 3

Read the following passage carefully and the instructions that follow it.

One day you were passing your principal's office when you saw a student knocking at the door, and carrying a large brown envelope. This person appeared to be either excited or a little frightened. You heard the principal's voice saying, 'Come in.' The student hesitated, glanced at the envelope and entered the office.

Explain to a friend, in detail:

- the appearance of the student
- why the student was seeing the principal
- what was in the envelope
- what happened during the interview
- what happened eventually to the student and the envelope

Exercise 4

You arrived early at school one day. You were the first person to enter your classroom. You saw immediately that during the night serious damage had been done.

Write an account describing what you saw and what action was taken to discover who caused the damage.

Use the following points and add your own details whenever possible:

- broken furniture
- damaged walls
- books torn
- litter on the floor
- enquiries made

Exercise 5

You were in a shop when you saw a person taking articles from a shelf and hiding them in a bag. You realised that the person was stealing.

Later, you were asked to write an eyewitness report for the police of what happened.

Write your report, based on the questions below, and adding details of your own.

- what did the person look like?
- what articles were taken?
- what part did you play in the incident?
- what did others in the shop do?
- how did the thief escape?

Exercise 6

When you were walking along the road, a child dashed out of a shop and knocked into a woman who was carrying a heavy basket. Her goods fell to the ground. There was an argument and a struggle. A crowd gathered. A policeman and the child's parents arrived.

Describe the scene in detail to the child's parents, including the following points and adding details of your own:

- the accident itself
- what various people said
- what various people did to help
- what the outcome was
- how the child reacted to the experience

Exercise 7

A young man riding a motorcycle crashed in a busy shopping area. He accused a student of causing the accident. You witnessed the event, seeing the following:

- a group of students
- a girl stepping onto the road
- loss of control
- the crash
- injuries

Write your account of the incident, mentioning all of the above points and adding details of your own. Make clear that the student was not to blame.

Exercise 8

The following letter has appeared in the newspaper:

Dear Sir,

Two days ago a bunch of noisy teenagers knocked my briefcase and my radio out of my hands as I was boarding a bus. They pushed me aside and shouted rude words at me.

Isn't it about time the parents and the school did something to cure the bad manners of students who race about the streets, untidily dressed, insulting people? They have too much freedom and spare time and are always causing trouble. They never think of others.

All young people should be more severely disciplined, have less money and be made to do something useful to keep them off the streets.

Yours faithfully,

A Beta

You feel strongly about the points made in the above letter. Write your reply in the form of a letter to the newspaper.

Include the following points and add details of your own where appropriate:

- sympathy for A Beta
- whether it is the school or parents' job to control teenagers or not
- whether teenagers are inconsiderate or not
- whether they have too much money and spare time
- whether teenagers should be made to do something useful

Exercise 9

A television company would like to make a programme about your school. The producer wants to film teachers and students at work, not the buildings and grounds. Your principal has asked you, as a senior student, to suggest the people and activities to be covered and to explain in detail why you think they should be included. Write your response in the form of a letter to the principal. You should include the following, making sure you add details of your own:

- your sense of pleasure at being asked to complete this task
- the best choice of a clever student to film
- the best example of a student who is good at sports
- a student noted for community efforts
- an example of teachers and pupils working at some project together

Unit 3
Comprehension

Introduction

This part of the book will deal with the comprehension paper. In this paper you will be tested on your ability to:

- select facts from a simple area of the passage
- select facts from a more complex area of the passage
- select key ideas from the passage and express them in your own words
- make simple deductions from various contexts in the passage
- rephrase words and expressions from the text

The chapters that follow will give you practice in assessing the different types of questions and how important it is to read the questions carefully. Don't begin your answer to a question until you are sure you have understood what it is asking you to do.

The range of questions will give you practice, too, in tackling the more difficult sections of the paper. Again, the technique of recognising what you have to do is all-important.

Golden rule

Always read the question carefully!

2 Simple questions on facts

In this chapter you will learn to recognise questions that test your ability to select simple facts from the passage. You will not be expected to rewrite these facts in your own words. It will be enough to write out the facts that you think answer the question.

This is what you should do:

❶ Read the question very carefully.

❷ The question will tell you which part of the text to study. Make sure that you go to that part of the text.

❸ Look for key words or phrases in the question that will lead to the facts you have to select.

Printed below are the opening lines of a passage about a school that is threatened by rising flood waters. Read the lines carefully and then look at the question that is set on them.

The floods stretched as far as the eye could see and the water was still rising. The headmaster was confident that the school had solid foundations and that there was no fear of the flood destroying the building. However, as he looked out at the old stone warehouse opposite and saw the water up to its second-floor window, he knew time was running out.

Question
In the opening paragraph above we learn that the headmaster was sure that the school building would not collapse. What made him so sure? [1]

As you read the question, you will see that an important word is repeated, namely the word 'sure'. You have to find out from the text why the headmaster was so sure the school would not collapse.

The word 'sure' does not actually occur in the text, but there is another word meaning much the same – 'confident'. This leads you to the reason why the headmaster was sure the building would not collapse.

Answer
The school had solid foundations.

Here is another question of similar difficulty. It is based upon the lifestyle of elephants in Burma. Printed below are the opening lines of the passage. Read the lines carefully and look at the question that follows them.

As civilisation eats into the jungle of south Burma with its roads, railways and airstrips, the herds of elephants grow fewer. Fortunately, there are vast forests in the north of Burma into which the herds will gradually withdraw, and for a long time to come find a peace that is characteristic of the jungle.

Question
What causes elephants to decrease in south Burma?   [1]

This time, the important word in the question is 'decrease'. Notice, too, that the question is about south Burma. The meaning of 'decrease' is not difficult (to shrink, grow smaller). As you look at the text again you find the same idea in 'grow fewer'. Now you have zeroed in on the part of the text that holds the answer, namely the opening words of the passage. It is civilisation 'eating' into the jungle of south Burma.

How much do you need to write to answer the question? In effect, it's the idea of civilisation eating into the jungle that's the real cause. The references to roads, railways and airstrips aren't essential.

> **Answer**
> Civilisation is eating into the jungle of south Burma.

So far, you have looked at questions looking for a simple fact from the opening part of the passage.

You have seen how important it is to:

- read the question carefully
- find the key word, or words, of the question and relate them to the text, to zero in on the correct fact in the text

Golden rule

Read the question carefully. It has important words that zero in on the correct facts in the text.

Now practise on a couple more of these opening 'simple' questions. You will be given the right answer at the end of the questions. Then you will see some examples of wrong answers, and what caused them to be wrong.

Passage 1

It all began with a Chinese princess named Hsi-ling. One day in the palace gardens she noticed a small, grey worm on a mulberry tree, spinning threads around itself to make a covering. It was a common sight; China had millions of such worms. She suddenly remembered how such threads had been used for the delicate strings of musical instruments in the past. Could they not also be unravelled and woven into cloth for clothes? The threads were stuck together with a gummy substance. But perhaps they could be loosened in warm water, and then… At that moment she had glimpsed just what could be done with that little grey worm. The silk industry was born.

Question
What suddenly gave the princess the idea that the threads of the grey worm could be unravelled and used for making clothes?   [1]

Notice the key words in the question: 'suddenly gave the idea that the threads could be used…'. 'Suddenly' links with 'suddenly remembered' in the text. The words 'could be used' link with the 'use of threads' for musical instruments.

> **Answer**
> She remembered the threads had once been used to make the strings of musical instruments.

The 'wrong' answer would be that there were millions of such worms in China. That doesn't concentrate on the idea of a 'use'. It would be wrong, too, to refer to the way the threads could be loosened in water. The question asks, 'What suddenly gave the princess the idea that…'. 'Loosening the threads' was not the first idea the princess had.

Golden rule

Only use the relevant part of the text!

Passage 2

A young boy has been hiding in some hills after his home had been seized by local bandits. He wants to find out if any of his family have survived.

Francis stepped cautiously out of the cave and peered through the darkness of the night in the direction of his home. Everywhere was silent except for the soft murmur of the river down below. His first move would have to be straight down the side of the hill. The bushes would give him good cover from the eyes of the bandits; they were bound to be on the look out. Then he could make for the shelter of the tall reeds on the river bank. From there he hoped he could reach the ample cover of the gardens round his house without detection.

Question

Francis 'stepped cautiously out of the cave'. Why did he have to move so cautiously?   [1]

Notice that this question does not give a lead with key words to take you to the part of the text that supplies the answer. You have to read the paragraph carefully and then find the reason why Francis moves so cautiously.

Answer

The bandits would be on the look out.

Copying the whole of the sentence 'The bushes would give him good cover from the eyes of the bandits; they were bound to be on the look out' would not earn the mark, even though the 'look out' idea is correct. The question is about Francis' first movement in stepping out of the cave, and not about finding 'cover' in any bushes.

Can you think of an alternative answer that is based upon 'the bandits would be on the look out'? The alternative answer could begin:

Francis stepped cautiously so that...

Now complete it. You will find the answer in Chapter 8 of this unit.

So far you have studied questions calling for fact selection from the opening part of the paper. You will have noticed that the questions are not too difficult to answer if you follow some simple steps. Let's revise these steps:

❶ Read the question carefully.

❷ Look for clues in the wording that can take you to the part of the text where the answer lies.

❸ Use the text wording for your answer if you want to, unless you are told to write it in your own words.

❹ Do not copy whole blocks of text, hoping that it contains the correct information somewhere. Use only the relevant part of the passage.

Practice session

Here are some straightforward tests of fact selection. Work on them by yourself. The answers are provided in Chapter 8 of this unit.

Don't be tempted to peep at the answers first before you try the questions!

Exercise 1

> I passed through the Peruvian customs with little or no difficulty and entered the Republic of Ecuador through a small village. The officials there were very kind and helpful. They wished me luck on my journey, and I set off into the jungle beyond. Ahead of me lay a narrow track, no doubt made by animals and occasional vehicles. It had deep ruts in it, and on every side the track was hemmed in by the fast-growing tropical undergrowth. Driving very slowly, and with careful manoeuvring, I moved along, keeping my wheels out of the deeper ruts.
>
> **Question**
> Why did the driver of the car have to go 'very slowly'?   [1]

The next question comes from a passage describing the growth of tourism and foreign travel. Note that the question asks, 'what is the reason…'. This means you must give only one reason.

Exercise 2

> Years ago 'tourism' was a word rarely used by most people. Today it is understood by people the world over. Foreign travel is taken for granted as part of holidaymaking. Consequently, this has become a major business. It has created a vast number of jobs, and it is currently estimated that in some countries one in five persons is employed in work related to the tourism industry.
>
> **Question**
> From the evidence of this paragraph, what is the reason to account for the rapid growth of tourism?   [1]

The next passage describes how modern travel has made the world seem a much smaller place. The question asks how modern travel has brought this about.

Exercise 3

For those who make journeys across the world, the speed of travel today has turned countries into a series of villages. Distances between them appear no greater to a modern traveller than those which once faced men as they walked from village to village. Jet planes fly people regularly from one end of the earth to the other. Man has now become a world traveller.

Question

Distances between countries no longer appear very great to travellers using the jet plane. What, according to this paragraph, is the reason for this?   [1]

3 More difficult questions on facts

In this chapter you will find more questions testing your ability to select relevant facts from the text. However, they will be more difficult than the previous examples in Chapter 2. Also, some of these questions will carry two marks.

Nevertheless, the techniques that you learnt in tackling the questions in Chapter 2 will help you with these more difficult ones.

Remember:

❶ Read the question carefully.

❷ Make sure you go to the right part of the text. Look for key words in the question that can help you to find it.

❸ Don't simply copy out whole blocks of text. Select the part that you think contains the answer.

In the questions that follow, you will have to read several lines of text to find the relevant facts. Examine the wording carefully. Look for details in the wording of the question that can take you to the relevant area of the text.

Here is the first of these more difficult questions. It comes from a passage about cats and how they found their way into people's homes and lives.

Passage 1

> The cat is a beautiful and graceful animal, and often the special friend of lonely people. It has had a long history in our lives. The ancient Egyptians were probably the first to domesticate the creature, and in fact gave it a special role among their gods. No doubt because of this special respect cats had earned, they were jealously guarded by the Egyptians. Their export was forbidden for at least a thousand years after they found their way into Egyptian homes and temples. Eventually, though, cats made their way east and west as the trade routes opened up and traders smuggled them out, some to Europe, others far afield to China, and then on to Japan.
>
> **Question**
> The Egyptians forbade the export of cats. How did they eventually make their way out of Egypt?   [1]

What are the important words in the question about cats? They are:

- the Egyptians 'forbade' their export
- cats 'made their way' out of Egypt

Notice that the word 'forbade' takes you in the text to 'their export was forbidden'. Now you can examine the text in that area to see how cats 'made their way out of Egypt'. The wording of the passage gives you the answer in the sentence '… cats made their way east and west as the trade routes opened up and traders smuggled them out…'.

> **Answer**
> Trade routes opened up and traders smuggled them out.

You could have added the text details 'to Europe… to China… to Japan', but they aren't really necessary. The question concentrates on 'how' cats made their way out, not 'where to'.

However, it would have been wrong to have included the sentence beginning, 'Their export was forbidden for at least a thousand years…'. The question does not ask for details about the history of their forbidden export.

Golden rule

Don't copy blocks of text. Choose the relevant details.

The question below comes from a passage describing a journey in the vast desert of southern Arabia. Note that the question carries two marks.

Passage 2

> At first light, we set off, anxious to push on while the air was still cool. Soon, huge hills of sand began to appear up ahead. One vast hill, well over 300 metres high, with a sheer, steep face, blocked our path.
>
> Muhammad, our guide, went ahead to reconnoitre. He looked confident enough, but I despaired of getting our camels up that steep cliff of sand. The rest of our party began to grumble out loud. 'No camel will climb that. We'll have to find a way round. We should have gone west to start with. It's all Muhammad's fault.' I sensed a growing jealousy that Muhammad was acting as their guide, but I kept silent. Any reaction on my part could easily provoke a quarrel, and that would make things ten times worse.
>
> **Question**
> The travellers grumbled that Muhammad had led them into trouble. What did the author believe was the *real* feeling behind this grumbling?   [2]

You have to read the whole of the section to find out what the 'trouble' is that the travellers are facing.

The word 'grumbled' takes you to the part of the text that refers to Muhammad. The word 'real', set in italics in the question, indicates that the travellers have another reason for 'grumbling', apart from the 'trouble' they were facing. The emphasis placed on 'real' should make you look further, to find the reason behind this grumbling. It is the feeling of jealousy.

You have to write out what they were actually 'jealous' of, that is, Muhammad acting as their guide. Simply writing 'they were jealous of Muhammad' would not be enough.

> **Answer**
> The travellers were jealous of Muhammad acting as their guide.

The next question comes from a passage about travel, comparing the advantages and disadvantages of journeys by boat, train and plane. Note that the question is worth two marks.

Passage 3

> The modern revolution in travel has possibly gone too far. A price has to be paid for the rapid conquest of time and distance. Yet travel is something to be enjoyed, not endured. The boat offered time and leisure enough to appreciate the sights and sounds of a journey, often with a comfortable living on board. A journey by train, too, still has a special charm about it. The scenery sweeping past your carriage window lulls you into a gentle state in which time and distance mean nothing. On board a plane, however, there is just the blank blue of the sky filling the narrow windows of the aircraft cabin. The soft lighting, in-flight films and canned music make up the only world you know, and the hours plod slowly by. It is a monotonous imprisonment.
>
> **Question**
> The author believes that travel by aircraft is 'monotonous'. What two things create this feeling of monotony for him?   [2]

Firstly, you can use the key word 'monotonous' to locate the relevant area of the text for your answer. Then you can examine the details about travel by plane which 'create the feeling of monotony'. 'Monotony' has the idea of a continuing 'sameness', with no variety to it.

One thing that creates the 'monotony' is the 'blank blue of the sky'. 'Blank' suggests there is nothing to see, nothing to provide interest. The other element must be the way time moves so slowly when there is nothing to see or do. So you select the expression, 'the hours plod slowly by'.

> **Answer**
> There is nothing to see from the plane except the blank blue of the sky, and also the hours plod slowly by.

The essential ideas are: there is nothing to see but the sky, and time goes very slowly. They earn the two marks for this question. But you do not have to reword the text expression. You can copy it directly.

Any additional detail from the text about boat or train travel would be irrelevant. It has nothing to do with the 'aircraft' of the question. It would deny any mark you might have gained for the 'monotony' element.

Practice session

> Some more of these tests of fact selection now follow for you to practise on. The answers are provided in Chapter 8 of this unit.

Don't be tempted to peep at the answers first!

The passage below comes from an imaginary story about the mysterious creature of the Himalaya mountains – the Abominable Snowman or Yeti – and of its fascination for a young girl named Lha-mo.

Exercise 1

One morning Lha-mo was far from home, searching for some animals that had strayed from the camp. The snow had begun to fall. Suddenly she stopped, startled. There in the snow were some enormous tracks, quite unlike those of any normal animal. Besides, this creature walked on two feet, not four. Was it a Yeti? She made up her mind to follow it, alone. There was no time to fetch anyone else; she was already far from the camp. Despite any fear she might have had of this unknown creature, she simply had to follow it. Also, the snow was covering its tracks fast. If she was to discover where it lived it must be now, at once.

Question
'She made up her mind to follow it.' Give two reasons why Lha-mo decided she had to go on at once.   [2]

Remember that the words in the question can take you to the relevant part of the text.

The next passage describes the intense heat of summer days in the countryside, and how a farmer and his wife react to it. The question concentrates on the reaction of the farmer.

Exercise 2

That summer the heat was intense. The grass had turned brown.
When the wind stirred, the corn rustled like paper flags. The farmer
and his wife noticed for the first time many more insects; they were
no doubt enjoying the heat that had encouraged them to breed.
Despite the high temperature, the farmer went about his usual work
looking after the cattle, as though they were the only thing of
importance. However, his wife kept on looking at the sky, waiting, it
seemed, for something ominous to happen.

Question
The farmer seems unconcerned by the 'intense heat'. What makes
him seem 'unconcerned'?   [1]

The passage on the next page centres on the behaviour of crocodiles
and the danger they can present to unwary people or animals.

The question says 'Explain fully why...' and has a mark weighting of
two marks. The combination of 'fully' and the mark weighting
indicates that that you must offer two reasons in your answer.

Exercise 3

Without doubt, the crocodile is one of the most dangerous creatures in Africa. Perhaps it is this reputation that attracts so many tourists. But you can never get close to one. As soon as you approach within 30 or 40 metres, it waddles away into the water and disappears. It is in the water, though, that it is at its most dangerous. Never stand too close to a river bank, especially at dusk. The chances are that a crocodile is lying nearby, submerged in the shallows, carefully observing you. Then with one sudden scythe-like movement of its tail it will sweep you into the water. It is no rare thing for a baby elephant, coming to the river to drink, to be killed in this way, while its mother rushes helplessly up and down the bank.

Question
Explain fully why 'dusk' is an especially dangerous time to stand close to a river bank in some parts of Africa.   [2]

The final question comes from a passage about the difficulties involved in photographing wild animals.

Exercise 4

Filming wild animals is extremely difficult. The photographer must get much closer than 200 metres if he wants a lifelike shot. This demands considerable junglecraft, and he must remain constantly downwind of the animal so that it is unaware of his presence. He must have a thorough knowledge of the animal's habits so that he will know where to find it and which way it is likely to move. All this demands enormous powers of patience and endurance. Often, after a long, exhausting wait in the blazing sun, he will in the end be outwitted by the animal's keener senses, and watch helplessly as it scampers off.

Question
The photographer's 'thorough' knowledge of an animal's habits does not always give him an advantage over it. Why not?   [2]

4 Answers in your 'own words'

This chapter will look at questions very similar to those appearing in Chapters 2 and 3. Once again, you will be expected to examine a short run of text and select key facts from it.

However, there is one important difference. You will have to present the relevant facts for the answer in your own words. You will always be prompted to do this by the question format, such as, 'You must answer in your own words'.

Only the relevant facts have to be presented in your own words. You may copy other wording from the text to 'frame' your answer. However, you will gain no reward for relevant facts if you lift them straight from the text.

The following passage describes how early man was committed to a wandering way of life:

Passage 1

> Travel in one form or another has always been a fundamental part of human life. Our earliest ancestors regularly pursued slowly moving herds of animals across the vast plains, for these animals were their prey, whose flesh ensured their very existence. This bred an instinct in early men that kept them always on the move, and in their endless wanderings they were perhaps pointing the way for the modern traveller of today.
>
> **Question**
> An 'instinct' kept early men on the move. Explain fully in your own words what bred this instinct in them. [2]

Note how the wording of the question, 'instinct' and 'kept early men on the move', takes you to the part of the text describing men following the herds of animals.

Examine the wording of the question, 'what bred this instinct', and you see that it comes down to 'what made men behave like this'. There are two marks for the question. You have to 'explain fully', and so two key ideas are required.

Remember, important words in the question can help you zero in on the right part of the text. The facts in the text are that men pursued animals as their prey.

So far, you have been adopting the same techniques that you practised in Chapters 2 and 3. You have used the wording of the question to help you locate the essential part of the text, and you have lined up facts that are relevant to the question: men pursued animals as their prey.

You now must tackle the final part of the question, that is, putting the essential facts in your own words. For 'pursue' you can substitute a word like 'follow' or 'go after'. 'Prey' suggests 'killing' or 'hunting down'.

Your answer then becomes:

> **Answer**
> The fact that men were always following animals to kill them.

The material in the text, 'across vast plains', does not stand as a key idea. It is only 'colouring' description, and you do not have to offer your own words for it. Also, you don't have to include 'whose flesh ensured their very existence'. This only expands the idea of 'prey'.

The following table outlines the essential elements of the task. It will also help you to remember that there are two sides to the 'own words' question. You have to:

- select the key facts from the text
- present them in your own words

Key facts from text	Substitution
men pursued animals as their prey	men followed animals to kill them

Passage 2

Here is another 'own words' question. This time it comes from a passage about the Great Wall of China, and how important it was to maintain it in China's early history.

The Great Wall of China grew out of a series of walls, built to keep marauding bandits away from cultivated farm lands. Eventually these walls were linked up to form the Great Wall itself. Nevertheless, it did not prevent trade between the farming communities and the peoples to the north of them. Indeed, as the farmers became more prosperous, their interest in the Great Wall as a defence began to wane, and they had become critical, too, of its construction.
Inevitably the Great Wall fell into disrepair and Genghis Khan and his Mongol armies were able to sweep into China and occupy large stretches of it.

Question

Explain fully in your own words why the farmers lost interest in the Great Wall as a means of defence.   [2]

Golden rule

Note the mark weighting for the question. Find the essential facts. Present them in your own words.

Use the key words 'interest... as a defence' to take you to the relevant part of the text. Note the mark weighting of two marks, and that you have to 'explain fully'. You will therefore need to provide two elements in your answer.

The two elements behind the farmers' 'lost interest' are: they became prosperous and critical of the Great Wall's construction.

Key facts from text farmers became prosperous were critical of the construction	*Substitution* farmers became wealthy disapproved of its being built

Answer
The farmers became wealthy and disapproved of building the Great Wall.

Practice session

Some more questions requiring answers in your own words now follow. You will find the answers to them in Chapter 8 of this unit.

The first question comes from a passage about a journey in Malaysia by elephant, and how difficult it can be to make an elephant obey you.

Exercise 1

> The elephant had been allowed to rest and take a bath in a nearby river. He threw large quantities of water over himself, and then plastered himself with mud from the river's edge for protection against insects. I clambered on his back again, and we rode for another two hours, yet at a cruelly slow pace. The elephant seemed determined to lie down at every possible moment. He roared when he was asked to go faster, sometimes with a roar of rage, sometimes in loud distress. In despair, the driver got off and walked behind him but at that point the elephant stopped altogether. In the end I had to walk the remaining stage of the journey to Kwala Kangsa.
>
> **Question**
> The elephant roared when he was prompted to go faster. Using your own words, say what two emotions the elephant appeared to be feeling when he roared.   [2]

The following passage comes from the story we saw earlier in Chapter 2, about the young boy whose home had been seized by bandits. Under cover of darkness, he is trying to get back into the gardens.

Exercise 2

> Francis snaked across the last patch of open ground and burrowed deep into the bushes around the base of a fig tree. Suddenly there came the crunch of boots on gravel: then silence. Francis sensed that the men were stealing towards him. The next moment a deafening volume of sound assailed Francis from all sides as the men closed in, beating the undergrowth with the butts of their rifles. Seconds later they beat at the branches and leaves above Francis. The broad leaves of the tree soaked up the blows and did not reveal any sight of their refugee below. There was another spell of frantic beating, and then the boots moved on. Francis trembled with relief.
>
> **Question**
> Using your own words, state two ways in which the fig tree saved Francis. [2]

The last passage comes from a description of a hazardous end to a journey by ferry boat on a river in Africa. The officers struggle to bring the boat under control as it is about to reach the dock.

Exercise 3

The dockers had attempted to get hold of the boat's heavy rope to secure it to the quay side, but the officers shouted at them to let it go. The boat had suddenly started to move backwards out to sea. What was the captain up to? The chief engineer decided to take control of the boat himself. He stopped the boat's engines and then sent it ahead once more, straight for a sandy stretch of beach alongside the quay. By now the passengers were in a frenzy of impatience to get off, and were running from side to side of the vessel. This created instability in the vessel, and only added to the general chaos. Finally, the chief engineer manoeuvred the boat close enough to the quay side for the dockers to get hold of its mooring rope and secure the wayward vessel.

Question
The passengers were impatient to get off the boat. Explain in your own words two dangerous effects of their impatience.   [2]

Chapters 2–4 have concentrated on questions dealing with the selection of facts. The techniques for tackling these questions have remained the same in these three chapters. They are:

❶ Read the question carefully.

❷ Use the wording of the question to take you to the part of the text where the answer lies.

❸ Do not copy whole blocks of text, hoping that somewhere it contains the correct information. Use only the relevant part of the passage.

In addition, you have seen the same sort of questions involving the use of own words. Remember that if you have to answer in your own words, the relevant facts must not be set in the text expression. You must substitute them with your own words.

5 Questions involving deductions from the text

In this chapter you will be practising questions that call for straightforward deductions from the text. Questions of this type do not require any extra knowledge outside of the text. All you have to do is study the relevant area of the passage and then 'read into' the text to find the answer. You will then be making a 'deduction' from the text.

The first question you will be looking at comes from a passage about the domestication of wild animals, and how their physical features gradually changed over time.

Passage 1

> One of the results of the domestication of wild animals was a gradual but distinctive change in their physical appearance. Most became smaller because Man could not cope with large animals or feed them as effectively as they fed themselves in the wild. Some animals, who were the natural prey of others, had been drab and undistinguished in colour. Over a long period of time their domestication produced more distinctive markings on them and brighter colours, as the need for camouflage disappeared.
>
> **Question**
> Why do you think some animals originally needed to 'camouflage' themselves? [2]

Notice that the question is worth two marks. Your answer will need two relevant details in it.

As you read the question, note that the key idea to consider is 'camouflage'. When you look around the area in the text where the word 'camouflage' appears, you will see a reference to the way animals had been 'drab and undistinguished in colour'. You will then realise that 'camouflage' is linked with this 'drab' colouring, when the animals were still in the wild.

Why did they need to be 'drab' and undistinguished'? So that they would not be seen easily as the 'prey' of other animals.

Answer
So that the animals that hunted them could not see them.

The two important elements are 'the animals that hunted them' and 'could not see them'. An answer which simply said 'so that they could not be seen' would be incomplete, and would not score both marks.

Here is that question again: 'Why do you *think* some animals originally needed to 'camouflage' themselves?'

You will see that the word 'think' is asking you to work out the reason why animals needed to camouflage themselves.

Very often you can recognise these 'deduction' questions by their wording. Here are some examples:

- 'Why do you think that...'
- 'Suggest a reason why...'
- 'What is so surprising about...'
- 'Why might it be difficult to...'

If you see a question phrased along these lines, you can be sure that you are expected to read beyond the surface meaning of the text and work out the answer.

Of course, it is not possible to give whole lists of phrases that introduce these 'deduction' questions. You must study questions carefully every time, and see how they relate to the text. Then you will be able to see whether the facts required for the answer come directly from the text, or whether you have to get 'behind' it to work out the answer.

However, you will never be expected to have any special knowledge to answer these 'deduction' questions. All you have to do is study the text carefully to work out the answer.

The examples so far show that the technique for answering 'deduction' questions has clear-cut stages to it. They are:

❶ Read the question carefully.

❷ Look for the lead it gives to the relevant text area.

❸ Work out what information you have to 'deduce' from that area of the text.

❹ Check the mark weighting of the question. This will decide the amount of detail necessary for the answer.

Another example of a 'deduction' question now follows, including a breakdown of the stages in answering it. The question comes from a passage about parachute jumping and why it seems a surprising sort of sport.

Passage 2

> Psychiatrists, it seems, are very interested in the motives of people who deliberately throw themselves out of aeroplanes, attached to something that to most of us appears flimsy and insecure. No one goes to the edge of a cliff and peers over without sensing the fear of taking one further step. Automatically, you pull back. To make a parachute jump you have to cross that gap, and push your mind through a protective barrier of fear. It is a move that is at odds with our basic instincts. Yet people take it voluntarily.
>
> **Question**
> Why should parachute jumping be considered 'at odds with our basic instincts'?   [2]

The question is worth two marks. Your answer should contain two essential details.

The words, 'at odds with our basic instincts', direct us to the relevant area of the text. The word 'fear' is nearby, which is an 'instinct'. Next, examine the words, 'at odds with'. This means 'contrary to' or 'fighting against'. As you read round this area you can work out that parachute jumping means that you 'fight' the 'fear' instinct.

> **Answer**
> Because parachutists have to fight against their instinct of fear.

The two important elements are fighting against the instinct, and the instinct is fear.

The next example of a 'deduction' question comes from a description of a journey by an open boat down the mighty river of India, the Ganges. At one point, the river becomes very shallow, and threatens to halt the progress of the boat.

Passage 3

> For more than an hour I had managed to keep the boat in the centre of the stream where there was just about enough water to keep us afloat. Suddenly luck was on our side, or so it seemed; the current gathered speed beneath us. Then ahead we saw the river beginning to foam and froth, and just discernible in the raging water, a second channel leading off to the side. Before we could do anything, we were sucked violently into its narrow entrance, thundering downwards in a sort of gorge, barely three metres wide. A strange excitement gripped us; our crew yelled and shrieked in a crazy sort of triumph while we were swept onwards downhill.
>
> **Question**
> The crew 'shrieked in a crazy sort of triumph'. Why do you think
> their triumph was crazy?   [1]

Notice that this question is worth one mark. You have to offer only one basic idea.

Now examine the words, 'shrieked in a crazy sort of triumph'. When you read round those words in the text, you see that the crew are hurtling helplessly down a narrow gorge. Next, consider the word 'triumph'. This usually suggests some sort of success. Here the crew were excited by the way the boat had gathered speed, after the earlier slow progress. Why was it 'crazy' to feel this 'triumph'? You must look at the whole situation to work this out. Clearly, being out of control in such a narrow gorge was highly dangerous, or even life-threatening. It was therefore 'crazy' to feel 'triumphant' about it.

> **Answer**
> Because they were in a very dangerous situation *or* because their lives were in danger.

It would not be enough to say that they were being 'swept onwards downhill', simply copying the original text. This does not pinpoint the danger that makes the 'triumph' a 'crazy' feeling.

Practice session

> More questions now follow requiring deductions from the text. You will find the answers to them in Chapter 8 of this unit.

The first question comes from a description of cattlemen, and how they used to drive their beasts in vast herds across the countryside in Europe.

Exercise 1

> Many years ago cattlemen in Europe drove vast herds of cattle along broad grassy tracks searching for fresh pasture. Often their own land was not rich enough to feed their cattle and so they were forced to look for new grazing. At times they encountered hostility from the local people who lived near the routes taken by the cattle. Therefore the cattlemen tried to follow dry, high land, avoiding swamps and the danger of surprise attack. Fattening their cattle was at times a risky business.
>
> **Question**
> Why should a high route prevent a surprise attack on the cattlemen?
>
> [1]

The next question is about the sudden increase in America of a species of ant called the 'fire-ant'.

Exercise 2

> North America is being invaded. It is a large-scale assault, with advance troops being landed on the southern shores to begin with, and then slowly pushing north on a broad front. The Americans are putting up a heroic resistance, but the enemy is advancing steadily. The invaders are ants, small, seemingly innocuous insects, commonly known as fire-ants. Their name comes not from the fiery-red colour of their bodies but from the intense, burning agony produced by their bite. These invaders also have a secret weapon: they breed rapidly and so can spread with frightening quickness.
>
> **Question**
> The 'invasion' of North America is described in dramatic, military language. What makes this choice of language so surprising?   [2]

Golden Rule

Look for a lead to the relevant text area. Read the text around it to work out your answer.

The following passage is from a description of a journey by raft across the Pacific Ocean to the islands of the South Seas. The author describes what happens when he finds a shark on the end of his fishing line.

Exercise 3

Suddenly the line snapped tight. This fish was pulling strongly, and going down. It felt like a shark. Now I didn't particularly want to catch a shark, but I wanted my hook back. Hauling hard on my line, I somehow managed to get it halfway up across the end of the raft. Then it thrashed so fiercely that I was thrown off balance, headfirst into the sea. When I straightened up to see where I was, the raft was already sailing away from me. In one magical moment I took in all its beauty as it rose on the blue sea, sails spread out in the wind – my golden raft, sailing away…

Question

In one 'magical moment' the author 'took in' the beauty of the raft. Why might this seem a strange moment to be observing the beauty of the raft?   [2]

The writer of the passage below describes what happens when he is careless in trying to release a captured rattlesnake from its box.

Exercise 4

It took me some time to lever off a large section of the lid, for it was firmly nailed on. I then did a very foolish thing; I bent down and peered into the box. The snake was, of course, furious for having been cooped up so long. As my face appeared in the sky above him, he lunged upwards with an open mouth. I saw the blunt head flying upwards to meet my descending face. I had a vision of a pink mouth, moist and wide open, with fangs hanging down at the ready and seeming as big as a tiger's claws. I flung myself backwards in an astonishing leap, just in time.

Question

The fangs of the snake seemed 'as big as a tiger's claws'. What do you think made them look like this to the author?   [1]

Questions involving tests of language

In this chapter you will be practising questions that test your understanding of the language used in comprehension passages.

These tests can be set in a number of ways:

- You may have to select a word or phrase from the passage to show that you have understood its use in the context.
- You may be asked to rewrite a short phrase from the passage in your own words.
- You may have to explain the effect in the passage of certain words or phrases.
- You may be asked to complete a sentence from the text to show that you have understood its meaning.
- You will be given a list of words or phrases from the comprehension passage. You will have to offer alternative expressions for them, matching their meaning in the passage.

Samples of these questions are set in the pages that follow. Help will be given in the opening examples to emphasise the techniques you should adopt.

❶ Always look at the way the words or phrases set are actually used in the passage to work out their meaning.

❷ Do not just write down a meaning you have seen in a dictionary. It may not be quite the meaning that the word has in the context of the passage.

The first question comes from a passage about two men who are smuggling out a valuable cargo of silver in their sailing boat.

Passage 1

> The two men hoisted the sail on their boat and pushed it free of the jetty. It passed out between the almost invisible headlands into the darkness of the gulf beyond, gliding along with no more noise than if it had been suspended in air.
>
> **Question**
> The boat makes no sound as it leaves. Which one word in this paragraph emphasises this silent movement?   [1]

Notice the precise instruction. You have to select *one* word only. Answers offering more than one word will not be rewarded.

Examine the wording of the question closely. The emphasis is on 'silence'; 'makes no sound' and 'silent movement' make this clear. Also 'leaves' and 'movement' point to an action. Which one word describes the silent 'action' of the boat?

> **Answer**
> gliding

You will get no marks if you added, 'with no more noise than if it had been suspended in air'. The answer requires only one word.

Here is another question asking for the selection of a word from the passage being studied.

Passage 2

> The game reserve was an enormous park, and most of it was sealed off from the public. To reach this prohibited area, one had to pass through a control post. No one was allowed to live in the reserve, although its borders were crowded with people who formerly had their homes there. Only the warden and his armed rangers could legally enter the restricted area itself.
>
> **Question**
> The warden and his rangers were the only ones allowed to enter the 'restricted' area. Write down a single word from the paragraph which shows that other people were not allowed to enter.   [1]

The word 'restricted' is highlighted in the question. Read the paragraph again to make sure you understand what it is saying. It means that the area is 'limited' to certain people; others can't enter. Now you can look for a single word that tells you 'other people can't enter' the area.

Answer
prohibited

Don't be tempted by 'sealed off', even though it does convey the idea of 'prohibited'. It is a two-word expression, and would therefore score no marks. Always read and follow the question instructions carefully!

Let's look at another type of question that tests your understanding of language. This type asks you to rewrite a selected expression from the passage.

Here is an example from a passage about the risk of meeting pirates in the South China Sea.

Passage 3

> The next stage of my journey lay across a short stretch of the China Sea, but I was worried. It could still be long enough to encounter the pirates I had heard about. Down at the harbour I asked one of the seamen there how long my journey would take.
>
> 'About three days,' he replied.
>
> Three days? It seemed an age while dodging pirates, but the map showed that this was a reasonable length of time.
>
> **Question**
> The author says the journey seemed an *age while dodging pirates*. Explain what the words in italics tell you about his fears for the journey.   [2]

First of all, look at what the question is asking. You will see that you have to concentrate on the expression 'age while dodging pirates'.

Next, read the paragraph again. It's all about the danger of meeting pirates at sea. The longer you are at sea, the greater the risk! Now you can see the meaning behind 'age'. It means 'a long time'. The second part of the expression, 'dodging', is not too difficult to answer. Ideas like 'avoid' or 'get away from' fit the meaning in the text. These two features make up the two marks set for the question.

> **Answer**
> It would make the journey seem long, trying to avoid pirates.

Another type of language question asks you to examine the 'effect'
of a word or phrase in the passage. The 'effect' means the way a
word or phrase can emphasise the meaning of the text, or make it
more colourful.

Here is an example of this sort of question:

Passage 4

> The tall thistles, once dead, posed a real danger to the countryside
> during the long hot days. At any moment a careless spark might
> kindle a dangerous blaze and the dry, lifeless thistles would supply a
> deadly fuel. At such times the sight of smoke in the distance would
> cause every man to mount his horse and fly to the danger spot. An
> attempt to stop the fire would be made by making a broad path
> among the thistles, to prevent the fire travelling.
>
> **Question**
> Why does the author use the word 'fly' when he could have written
> 'ride'?   [1]

The question presents you with two words: 'fly' and 'ride'. You have
to explain why 'fly' seemed a better word to use.

Look at the text. It is all about the danger of fire in the countryside,
and how people react to it. They 'fly' to the danger spot. What does
that suggest? The idea of 'speed'. 'Ride' would not by itself do that.
In fact, it could suggest quite an ordinary pace.

Concentrate on the idea of 'speed' in your answer.

> **Answer**
> Because the author wants to describe the speed of the horsemen.

The next passage is about a river in flood after a great storm. The author is trying to escape from local villagers who have held him captive, and he risks a journey by raft down the river.

Passage 5

> I urged my raft into the swollen river. The lightning revealed a swirling mass of water, herding trees along in its rushing current. I knew it would be impossible to steer round them; the speeding water would be too much for me. I would have to try to bump and nudge my raft past them.
>
> **Question**
> The river is 'herding' fallen trees along in its current. What picture does the author create by using the word 'herding'?   [1]

The question asks you to suggest a 'picture' created by the word 'herding'.

What does 'herding' suggest in the first place? It's the idea of cattle. How does that fit into the description of 'trees'? Think of what cattlemen do when they 'herd' animals. They gather them together in a group. Read the passage again. 'Herding' gives a picture of the trees being gathered together like cattle.

> **Answer**
> The river is gathering the trees together.

When tackling questions that ask you to describe or explain the 'effect' of a word or phrase:

❶ Look carefully at the text to see its setting.

❷ Check to see what the question is asking you to do. You may have to describe a 'picture' created, or say why the word in the question is better than others with a similar meaning.

Questions can also test understanding of language by asking you to complete a sentence from the text with your own expression while keeping the original meaning.

An example follows below. It comes from a passage about a journey by train through Russia into the heart of China, and how the 'sameness' of the long journey has a strange hypnotic effect.

Passage 6

> Somehow the view of the passing scenery hypnotizes you. It never seems to vary. Even so, you cannot take your eyes away from the window in case there should be something outside you might miss. At last evening comes; you go on peering out into the endless forests sweeping by until the window shows you nothing but your face. It is time to try the dining car again. Will there be anything different there this time?
>
> **Question**
> 'the window shows you nothing but your face.' This phrase could be rewritten, with one word missing, as follows: 'the window shows you only the… of your face.'
>
> Write down the one word you think would complete the sentence, and which would keep the meaning of the original.   [1]

Of course, the first thing to do is to be sure of what the original sentence is saying. It means, 'You can only see your face in the window'. Look at the whole text. 'At last evening comes' tells you night has fallen. That accounts for the statement, 'the window shows you nothing but your face'. What would you see in the window? The… of your face. Now you can think of a word that would fit the situation and fill the gap above.

Answer
reflection

Here is another question of the same type. It comes from a description of a journey by elephant in Malaysia. You have already come across this passage in Chapter 4.

Passage 7

> An elephant is a truly strange beast, with its grey, wrinkled hide, huge ragged ears, and its trunk, which coils itself snakishly around anything that catches its curiosity or interest. I had always imagined elephants as being arrayed in rich cloth-of-gold trappings. My elephant had none of this. In fact there was nothing grand about him but his size.
>
> **Question**
> 'In fact there was nothing grand about him but his size.'
> This sentence could be rewritten with one word missing, as follows:
> 'The only thing that was… about him was his size.'
>
> Write down one word of your own which you think would complete the sentence, and which would keep the meaning of the original. [1]

The meaning of the original sentence is not difficult to follow. 'Nothing… but' is rewritten for you in the question wording as, 'The only thing that…' That is easy to understand.

That leaves the word 'grand' to substitute. Notice the instruction in the question: you have to write down one word of your own. You mustn't use 'grand' again!

Before you write down your word, try composing a sentence in the question format, filling in the gap, and keeping the sense of 'grand'. What does 'grand' suggest? Ideas of 'fine', 'splendid' or 'magnificent'. So, 'The only thing that was magnificent about him was his size' would convey a similar meaning.

> **Answer**
> 'magnificent'
> ('Fine' or 'splendid' would also be acceptable answers.)

Golden rule

Always look at the instructions carefully.

Often words or phrases are selected from the comprehension passage and you are asked to substitute equivalent words for them.

Here is an example of this type of test. The words and phrases are chosen from a limited area of text. In a full-size examination paper you can expect them to be chosen from the passage as a whole.

The text is from a passage describing locusts and the enormous damage they can do to the countryside.

Passage 8

Locusts usually fly in a compact mass near the ground, but it is
not uncommon for them to fly at great heights. The sure sign
of their approach is a sudden darkening of the sky to a brown
colour, creating a thick shadow over the earth. This soon
breaks up as blankets of the hungry insects descend upon the   5
land. There the swarms can do untold damage. Farmers watch
in utter hopelessness as the tiny beasts descend on their fields,
consuming everything – leaves, flowers, fruits and even the
stems of food crops. In minutes the keen appetite of these
creatures destroys the farmers' livelihood. The winged plagues   10
of the dreaded Desert Locust have the potential to affect an
estimated ten per cent of the world's population. Not only do
they go for the large-scale crops of commercial food producers
but also those of private farmers. People feel that something
must be done to stem these ravaging attacks before they get   15
out of hand.

Question
Choose *five* of the following words or phrases. For each of them,
give *one* word or a short phrase (of not more than *seven* words)
which has the same meaning that the word or phrase has in the
passage.

1. compact (line 1)	5. keen (line 9)
2. sure (line 2)	6. go for (line 13)
3. breaks up (line 5)	7. stem (line 15)
4. utter (line 7)	8. ravaging (line 15) [5]

Don't begin to answer this question until you have looked carefully
at the instructions. Let's take them one by one.

● You must choose only five of the words or phrases. Only the first
  five answers will be considered. Any excess answers will not be
  credited!

- You may offer one word or a short phrase for your answer. But notice the seven-word limit for a phrase.
- Do not offer a series of separate attempts at any one answer. Only the first attempt will be considered.
- Your answer must have the same meaning as the original word in the passage.

Now that you have looked carefully at the instructions, you can select the words or phrases for your answers.

Usually you will have a choice from a range of words or phrases, as in this question. It is therefore important to make your choice wisely. Check your choices as follows:

- Am I confident about the meanings of the words and/or phrases I have chosen?
- Am I sure that I know what they mean in the text?

If you are familiar with the words and/or phrases you are substituting, make sure that your substitutions carry the meaning that the original words and/or phrases have in the text. Do not quickly put down a half-remembered meaning from a dictionary.

To see how important it is to examine the meanings in the text, look at the phrase 'go for' from the question. This does not simply mean 'approach' or 'move towards' in the passage. It has the idea of 'concentrate on' or 'attack'. Similarly, 'stem' in line 15 has an altogether different meaning from the use of the word in line 9. In line 15 it means 'halt'.

As a further example, 'keen' in line 9 would not mean 'enthusiastic', which is a common meaning of the word. In the text it describes the appetite of the locusts as they devour the farmers' crops hungrily. So it must carry the sense of 'sharp' or 'acute'.

IIere are sample answers to all the words and phrases in the
question.

1.	compact	tightly packed
2.	sure	certain
3.	breaks up	scatters
4.	utter	complete
5.	keen	sharp
6.	go for	concentrate on
7.	stem	halt
8.	ravaging	destroying

We have already looked carefully at the instructions for the
question. Answers which ignore them can incur an expensive loss of
marks!

Remember to offer only one word or phrase in your answer.
Consider these two different attempts at 'go for' (number 6):

● attack
● approach, attack

The first one scores the mark, but the second doesn't, even though a
correct equivalent is present. It is offered as a second and separate
word. The comma marks the separation.

However, you can offer a phrase answer for one of the single words.
You could answer 'go for' as: concentrate on and attack. If you offer
a phrase answer like this, make sure the two words offered are
joined by 'and' to form a whole unit.

Try to keep the meanings of the two words in your phrase as close
as possible to the meaning in the text. You won't be rewarded for a
phrase answer if one of the words in it is wide of the mark.

Consider these two different phrase answers for 'breaks up' (number 3):

- scatters and goes away
- scatters and destroys

Obviously the second one would not score a mark. 'Destroy' is an entirely wrong idea.

You can write out the original word or phrase every time in line with your answer, or just assign the number it has in the question. But make sure that your numbering is accurate. A correct answer set against the 'wrong' number can't be rewarded!

In the next chapter, there are some questions for you to practise on. They will cover the different types of language tests we have seen in this chapter.

7 Practice questions on language

The practice questions that follow in this chapter are of the same pattern as those you saw in the last chapter. Take care to identify the different types of tests involved, and then apply the guidance you were given about them. The answers come in Chapter 8 of this unit.

Exercise 1

It is exciting to stand on a railway platform beside the great Trans-Siberian Express and to know that it is about to take you on eight days of solid travel. The tracks reach out into the distance: those eight days will carry you to the borders of China. You will have travelled continuously across one mighty continent to another, from west to east.

Question

The author is going to travel 'continuously' by train to the borders of China. Write down one word from this paragraph which carries the same idea as 'continuously'. [1]

Exercise 2

We set off down the River Ganges early in the afternoon. Ahead of us stretched a journey of 1800 kilometres all the way to the Bay of Bengal. Our steel-plated boat seemed sturdy enough for the demands we would make on it. It had taken 32 men to carry it down to the river from the boat shed. Its weight alone was a guarantee of its reliability.

Question

The weight of the boat was a 'guarantee of its reliability'. Explain what the author means by 'guarantee of its reliability'. [2]

Exercise 3

The great Industrial Revolution led to the establishment of large factories. This meant that workers had to be accommodated close to their place of work. Houses therefore had to be built quickly. Local authorities had no alternative but to throw up row upon row of cheaply-built dwellings. It was not long before the sooty smoke from the factory chimneys turned them into drab heaps of brick and tile.

Question

Local authorities had to 'throw up' houses quickly for the factory workers. Apart from the idea of speed, what else does 'throw up' tell you about the way these houses were built?   [1]

Exercise 4

The next morning we started our journey across the vast desert. We slowly made our way over one of the great hills of sand confronting us. On the way down, our leading camel, which carried the precious water skins, hesitated on the steep slope. I could see what was going to happen and shouted desperately to Muhammad. I was too late. The camel lost its balance and collapsed on top of the water skins. Muhammad ran over and slashed at the ropes that secured the water skins to the camel. If they had burst, our journey across the desert would have been over before it had properly begun.

Question

The author could have written 'Muhammad cut the ropes' instead of 'slashed at the ropes'. Why do you think he wrote 'slashed at'?   [1]

Exercise 5

> The hunter knew the leopard had him trapped. He lay there in abject terror, staring up at the bank above him. Ears flat, tail lashing, the leopard crouched above him, preparing to spring. Suddenly the hunter felt himself pushed roughly to one side, and then knocked flat on his back. Looking upwards, he saw standing over him a creature so enormous that his startled mind could not comprehend it. Then he saw a massive clawed foot, a wall of coarse hair, and a great muzzle outlined against the sky. It was a huge bear.
>
> **Question**
> The phrase 'startled mind' describes the mental state of the hunter. Complete the following sentence by inserting one word, which carries the same idea as 'startled'.
>
> The hunter was so … that he could not comprehend what he saw.
>
> [1]

On the next page is part of a passage describing the work of a wildlife photographer. You came across another section of this passage in Chapter 3, in handling questions on facts.

This time you will be practising the question that asks you to substitute your own expressions for words and phrases chosen from the text. Remember to look carefully at the way they are used in the passage. Don't just write down a half-remembered meaning you may have seen in a dictionary.

Exercise 6

Hunters often say that filming wild animals cannot compare
with hunting them. They claim that a tiger is at its most
treacherous when wounded and that a photographer does not
have to follow up a wounded animal as they often have to do.
Therefore in their eyes photography is a much less hazardous   5
business. Yet the hunter is far better equipped to deal with
treacherous animals than a photographer. If a photographer
suddenly encounters a tigress with cubs or an angry bear, he
has no powerful rifle as a safeguard. He would find it
impossible to take pictures if he burdened himself with such a   10
weapon.

Yet the rewards a photographer gains are infinitely superior to
those of a hunter. The skin of an animal or a pair of antlers on
a wall are scarcely works of art. They are merely personal
trophies to recall the hunt, and decaying ones at that. The   15
animal's coat soon loses its shine, and the antlers end up
looking like burnt twigs. But a good photograph can capture an
animal's movement or expression permanently, and in such a
way that everybody can enjoy the fruits of the photographer's
efforts.   20

Question

Choose *five* of the following words or phrases. For each of them,
give *one* word or a short phrase (of not more than *seven* words)
that has the same meaning that the word or phrase has in the
passage.

follow up (line 4)   gains (line 12)
hazardous (line 5)   merely (line 14)
encounters (line 8)   capture (line 17)
safeguard (line 9)   fruits (line 19)   [5]

You have now completed your practice on the range of questions testing various types of comprehension. The next section of this book concentrates on the summary question.

Before you tackle that section, you may want to see how well you did with the practice questions in Chapters 2 to 7. The answers are supplied in the following chapter.

8 Trial questions — answers

Answers	Marks
Chapter 2	
Passage 2 (Alternative answer)	
So that he would not be heard (or seen) by the bandits.	1
Chapter 2	
1 To keep the wheels of the car out of the deep ruts.	1
2 Foreign travel is taken for granted as a part of holiday making.	1
3 The speed of travel (has turned countries into a series of villages)	1
Chapter 3	
1 Because there was no time to fetch anyone else and the snow was covering the creature's tracks fast. (Zero marks for 'she was far from camp' alone or 'the snow was covering the tracks' without 'fast'.)	2
2 Because he is working as usual with the cattle.	1
3 Because a crocodile might suddenly sweep you into the water.	2
4 He could be outwitted by the animal's senses.	2
Chapter 4	
1 He was feeling angry and upset. ('upset' replaces the word 'distress' in the text. Also, ideas of 'pain' or 'discomfort' would do. 'angry' replaces 'rage'.)	2

Answers	Marks
2 It absorbed the beating and kept Francis hidden. ('absorbed the beating' replaces 'soaked up the blows' of the text. 'Kept … hidden' replaces 'did not reveal any sight'.)	2
3 It made the boat unsteady ('instability' in the text) and increased the confusion ('added to the chaos' in the text).	2
Chapter 5	
1 The cattlemen could see it coming.	1
2 Because the invaders are only (small) ants and apparently harmless.	2
3 Because he had fallen into the sea and the raft was drifting away from him.	2
4 Because the fangs (or the snake) were so close. (Or the idea that the author was frightened/alarmed.)	1
Chapter 7	
1 solid	1
2 The weight made sure ('guarantee') that it would last ('reliability').	2
3 In a poor or careless manner. (Or the idea of 'crudely'/'simply' built.)	1
4 To emphasise Muhammad's concern or fear for the safety of the water skins/to emphasise his speed. (Or the idea that Muhammad was desperate to free the water skins as quickly as possible.)	1
5 frightened or alarmed	1
6 *follow up:* go after *gains:* earns *hazardous:* dangerous *merely:* only *encounters:* meets *capture:* secure/fix *safeguard:* protection *fruits:* rewards (These answers are worth 1 mark each.)	

Unit 3 — Further practice

The questions in this chapter will give you practice on the range of questions that have appeared in Unit 3 as a whole. Take care to identify the different types of test involved and then apply the guidance you were given about them in the previous chapters of the unit.

The answers come later, following the sequence of the questions. *Don't peep at the answers before you do the questions!*

The first three questions come from a description of a journey to a remote corner of Central Africa – to the great national park of the River Congo.

Exercise 1

The air was hot. We had been travelling up the mighty River Congo and were now entering one of the world's last untouched tropical forests. Thunderstorms were beginning to sweep through the area, bringing great torrents of rain. All around, the forest steamed in the heat as we began marching through low-lying countryside, making for the interior of the forest.

Question
How had the writer made his way to the 'untouched tropical forest'?

[1]

Exercise 2

Suddenly a dozen chimpanzees came out of the forest on all sides. Yelling and dancing wildly on the branches, they bared their teeth at us, tore off the smaller branches and hurled them at us with surprising accuracy. We remained quite still, and kept quiet. Then just as suddenly as they had come, they left us. Clearly, our behaviour was reassuring; they did not regard us as a threat.

Question

What was it about the behaviour of the writer and his companions that 'reassured' the chimpanzees?   [1]

Exercise 3

After an exhausting morning's march, we had collapsed on the ground to rest. But our group leader was still pacing around, looking at his compass, consulting his map and putting us all to shame with his display of energy. Clearly, in such an unfriendly environment he accomplished so much because he was relentless.

Question

Explain *in your own words* why the leader was able to succeed in that 'unfriendly environment'.   [1]

The next questions come from a passage about kite flying and its origins in Asia.

Exercise 4

Kite flying has been popular throughout Asia for hundreds of years. Many of the kites are elaborately constructed, with a framework of bamboo and leaves, which makes a pleasant humming sound when the kite dives and weaves through the air. It seems like some brilliantly painted bird, alive with pleasure at being with other birds high up in the sky.

Question
What in particular makes a kite seem like a bird as it 'dives and weaves through the air'?   [1]

Exercise 5

Kites have even been used to carry men up into the air, though this could not be done when a strong and constant wind was blowing. There is a story about a Japanese thief who risked his life on a man-carrying kite in a daring attempt to steal gold from statues on top of a castle. Most of us, however, feel that nobody with his wits about him would willingly expose himself to such peril.

Question
Explain in *your own words* what, according to the author, prevents most of us from risking the perils of taking to the air in a kite.   [1]

Exercise 6

Kites played their part in the development of radio communication when aerials were fixed to them to carry early radio signals. Also, experiments with kites influenced the first designs of flying machines. When the air disturbance of some passing jet plane rattles the lines of high-flying kites, their owners on the ground smile approvingly; they know the history and potential of their elaborate creations.

Question
Explain the difference between 'history' and 'potential'.   [2]

The next few questions come from a passage describing a journey on horseback to a remote cattle ranch in Australia. In this part of the passage, the rider is confronted by a dangerous river that he has to cross.

Exercise 7

He rode up to the bank of the river. It was racing along in a mad jumble of debris, young trees, logs, and dead animals. He had swum across rivers on horseback many times, but never such a river as this. Besides, he was only too conscious of the limitations of the horse he was riding. He thought of how it had behaved on much of the journey so far, especially among the forest trees. It had swerved aside at everything and nothing.

Question
The horse on the journey so far had often 'swerved aside at everything and nothing.' What does this tell you about the horse? [1]

Exercise 8

Choosing a spot where the river bank shelved gently down to the water, he decided to brave the crossing. But the horse immediately fought with him in an effort to get back up the bank. He drove her forward again, and they plunged into the river. The water was icy cold, its chill striking to the bone. He was afraid of becoming so cold he would not be able to control the reins, and so he kicked his legs and shouted at the horse to encourage it. The unbelievably rapid current took hold and swept them along, out of control.

Question

Give two reasons from this section why it would have been dangerous for any horseman to have entered the river.   [2]

Exercise 9

Suddenly the swollen carcass of a kangaroo was swept towards the horse and rider. The horse swung away in panic and then suddenly turned completely over. Horse and rider were now underwater, fighting for life. The rider felt himself torn from his mount by the swirling current. Realising that his strength was fast running out, he struggled desperately to catch hold of the horse's reins.

Question

Why do you think the rider was so desperate to catch hold of the horse's reins?   [1]

The questions that follow come from a passage about Florence Nightingale. She was the first woman to organise proper nursing for British soldiers wounded in battle. She, along with her companions, left England in 1854 for the battlefields in southern Russia, but found that the army staff did not particularly welcome them.

Exercise 10

On their arrival from England, Florence Nightingale and her party of nurses were escorted to the military hospital with every appearance of flattering attention.

Question

What does 'every appearance' suggest about the 'flattering attention' they received?   [1]

Exercise 11

The English nurses were shown to their rooms – they were damp, filthy and unfurnished. Nor was any food officially laid on for them. Florence Nightingale realised this was a warning about any more flowery promises from those in authority back in England.

Question

What do you think was the 'warning' for Florence Nightingale about any promises made by officials in England?   [1]

Exercise 12

Wounded men began to pour into the hospital in numbers far too great for its scanty resources. Amidst the misery and confusion, the harassed doctors were forced to turn to Florence Nightingale and her nurses for help in the end.

Question

Explain *in your own words* what 'scanty resources' means.   [2]

The following questions are based upon a passage about a journey across the Sahara Desert to a lonely little town called Taoudenni. The questions centre on some of the dangers and difficulties of that journey.

Exercise 13

> Ahead of us lay the beginnings of a vast plain, dry and lifeless, a stern test of survival if ever there was one. But our impatience to be off drove out any anxiety we might have felt, and so we started in the bitter cold of the early dawn.
>
> **Question**
> What *two* reasons might have made the travellers 'anxious' as they gazed out on the vast plain?   [2]

Exercise 14

> We had not gone far when a wind sprang up. It began in gusts, coming over a great ridge of rock thay lay directly ahead. Soon it reached gale force, sweeping up the sand in clouds straight into our faces. The features of the plain were lost and the great ridge of rock disappeared.
>
> **Question**
> Explain how the combined effects of wind and sand could cause the 'disappearance' of the great ridge of rock.   [1]

Exercise 15

> The days that followed were spent toiling over range after range of
> sand dunes. The depressing nature of our journey compelled us to
> concentrate on little things just to stay mentally alive: here a soft
> patch of sand to avoid, a stone there to tread on. It was an
> exhausting monotony.
>
> **Question**
> What does 'exhausting monotony' tell you about the travellers'
> journey?   [2]

The passage that follows describes the mysterious stone statues that
stand in great numbers on Easter Island, a lonely spot way out in
the Pacific Ocean. The questions that are based upon it are similar
in style and content to those you have been practising already.

A walk among giants

❶ The story is told of a giant who waged war against the
islands in the Pacific Ocean. Armed with a huge iron bar, he
used it to lever up and gather together all the islands he
came to. He then flung them back into deeper water, where
they sank. Eventually he came to Easter Island. Although he   5
managed to break pieces off it to reduce its size, the
remaining core was particularly hard rock which resisted all
his efforts.

❷ Easter Island is the most remote inhabited place in the
entire world. No other island is further away in any direction   10
from the next nearest habitation: Pitcairn Island lies some
2200 kilometres to its west, and the South American coast
some 3700 kilometres to its east. All the rest is water. Not
surprisingly, the island is difficult to get to. Indeed, until an
airport was made in the 1960s, it was all but impossible,   15
because the only connection with the rest of the world was
a ship that visited the island once a year. There is now

something called a hotel on the island. Otherwise, many of
the islanders, who number about 2000, are keen to put up
visitors: there is always a crowd at the airport to meet   20
incoming planes and offer rooms and meals.

❸ The first shock that I received on reaching the island had
nothing to do with the stone figures I had come to see. It
was the sight of the island itself that filled me with
astonishment. It was so barren: there were no trees, and it   25
was apparent that scarcely any ground was good enough to
support crops or even much grazing. However, nobody
looked hungry or unhappy. The second shock left me in a
state of wonder. Many people have indeed seen
photographs of the enormous stone figures, but the pictures   30
show single statues or groups of only three or four. What I
now discovered was that there are hundreds: they are all
over the island. There are fully formed statues, plainly ready
to be taken away to their resting place, but there are also
huge unshaped 'logs' of rock, waiting to be attacked with the   35
stone axe, which was the only shaping tool the makers had;
and there are figures in every stage between. To wander
among them is a haunting experience. There is one in
particular, lying on its back, staring forever into the sky, that
fascinated me. I felt that if it had suddenly got up and   40
walked, I would not have been surprised.

❹ Every visitor must be mystified as to how the figures were
moved. They are massive, some more than 10 metres tall,
and weighing more than 80 000 kilos. Yet it seems that the
islanders, in the far-off days when these statues were made,   45
had not yet developed any sort of hauling machinery or any
kind of lifting gear. Still they managed to move these
immense, silent creatures over rough and, indeed,
unsmoothable masses of rock until they got them to the
stone bases prepared for them. Often they had to be   50
transported from the quarry over distances of up to 16
kilometres.

❺ Oh, if only the statues would get up and walk, provided that they talked as well! For a start, we might learn who they were, these long-dead carvers of stone. Did they come from an island to the west, or from South America to the east? No one knows. And when? Surprisingly, the experts can only offer us possibilities of dates extending from the 7th century to the 16th. No one knows. But the further we get into the mystery, the deeper becomes our ignorance. What were the statues? Were they gods to be worshipped? Were they monuments to ancestors? Were they used in rituals, ceremonies, offerings? No one knows. Beautiful and elaborately carved inscriptions have been found on them all over the island, and scholars have studied them for many years without succeeding in deciphering the signs and thus learning the language. What did these people want to say to us? No one knows.

❻ But the innermost mystery is this: apparently on one single day, a sudden destruction took place. In the quarry, tools were flung down; figures, from the finished to the hardly started, were deliberately toppled over. Throughout the island those that were in the process of being moved to their resting places were overthrown and abandoned at the point reached on their journey. Many theories have been put forward to account for this: invasion, mass hysteria, civil strife. The stone faces, with their impenetrable expressions, lying just where they were when disaster struck, still guard their secret. It seems that no amount of study will enable scholars to extract it from them, just as the giant in the folk tale failed to lever up the island's core of rock.

❼ Before disaster struck, the island was ringed right round its shores with those mighty stone bases, each bearing a line of statues. You could picture them as ranks of silent sentinels, placed there to defend the island from sea-borne foes. You would be wrong: every one of the figures — yes, every one — had its back to the sea.

You have read the passage about the giant statues on Easter Island. Now answer all the questions which follow below.

You are recommended to answer the questions in the order set.

From Para 1:
1. What defeated the attempt of the giant to 'lever up' Easter Island?   [1]

From Para 2:
2. (a) What has always made Easter Island difficult to get to?   [1]
   (b) 'There is now something called a hotel on the island.'
       What does the writer want you to understand about the hotel on the island?   [1]
   (c) Explain why a hotel was unnecessary before the 1960s.   [1]

From Para 3:
3. (a) Why did the writer expect to see people on the island who were hungry?   [1]
   (b) The writer received a 'shock' when he began to investigate the statues. Explain fully what caused this 'shock'.   [2]

From Para 4:
4. What *two* reasons make the fact that the statues were moved to their bases such a mystery?   [2]

From Para 5:
5. (a) The writer wants to know when the carvers of stone arrived on the island. What is surprising about the dates offered by so-called experts?   [1]
   (b) Scholars have tried to interpret the 'elaborately carved inscriptions' on these statues but failed. Give *two* reasons why their failure also strikes us as surprising.   [2]

From Para 6:

6. The writer refers in human terms to the statues when he
   writes about their 'impenetrable expressions'. What is he
   saying here?   [1]

From the whole passage:

7. Choose *five* of the following words or phrases. For each of them
   give one word or short phrase (of not more than *seven* words)
   which has the same meaning that the word or phrase has in the
   passage.

1. keen (line 19)	5. extending (line 58)
2. barren (line 25)	6. hardly (line 71)
3. fascinated (line 40)	7. account for (line 76)
4. offer (line 58)	8. ranks (line 84) [5]

From Para 7:

8. People might think the giant statues were some sort of
   magical defence against an attack from the sea. What could
   give them this idea, and why would it be wrong?   [2]

Answers to the questions on 'A walk among giants' appear on pages
219–220 of this chapter.

Answers to practice questions
on Exercises 1–15 of this chapter

	Answers	**Marks**
1	By the river Congo.	1
2	They kept still or quiet.	1
3	He never gave up/he never stopped working. (The word 'relentless' from the text has to be interpreted.)	1
4	Its humming sound.	1

Answers to practice questions (cont'd)

	Answers	Marks
5	We are too sensible to take such a risk. (The phrase from the text, 'with our wits about us', has to be interpreted.)	1
6	'History' refers to what has happened already while 'potential' refers to what could happen in the future.	2
7	It was nervous/frightened.	1
8	The water was icy cold and the current was unbelievably/extremely/tremendously rapid.	2
9	To stop being swept away by the current/so that the horse could save him. (The question tests an ability to make a deduction from the overall evidence of the paragraph. 'Why do you think…' is the clue to the type of question here.)	1
10	It was only a show/a pretence/not sincere. (The question tests an ability to interpret an implication, i.e. to get behind the phrase 'every appearance' and see what is really meant.)	1
11	Not to trust them/not to believe them. (The question tests an ability to make a deduction from the overall evidence of the paragraph. 'What do you think…' is the clue to the type of question here.)	1
12	The hospital's supplies/equipment/staff were small/meagre/limited.	2

Answers to practice questions (cont'd)

	Answers	Marks
13	The plain was dry/lifeless and they were afraid they would not survive/last in it.	2
14	The 'effects' prevented them from seeing/they blinded them. (The evidence of 'sweeping… sand in clouds… into our faces' has to be interpreted.)	1
15	It was tiring/wore them out and never varied/ was always the same.	2

'A walk among giants'

	Answers	Marks
1	Its hard rock/its core of hard rock.	1
2(a)	It is remote/the most remote place in the world.	1
2(b)	It is not much of a hotel/a hotel in name only. (The phrase from the text, 'something called a hotel', has to be interpreted.)	1
2(c)	A ship visited the island only once a year/visitors came only once a year.	1
3(a)	There was little ground to grow crops/food.	1
3(b)	Pictures had only shown three or four statues, but there were hundreds of them.	2
4	The islanders had no hauling machinery/ lifting gear and the statues had to be moved over rough rock.	2

Answers to practice questions (cont'd)

	Answers	Marks
5(a)	They cover such a wide span/appear so vague. (The span of dates in the text, 'from the 7th century to the 16th' has to be assessed in terms of 'experts'.)	1
5(b)	There were so many of the inscriptions and the scholars had studied them for so many years. (The evidence from the text, 'have been found all over the island' and 'for many years', points to the opportunity scholars had to study the inscriptions in depth.)	2
6	You cannot tell what they are thinking.	1
7	*keen:* eager *barren:* bare/unproductive/infertile *fascinated:* filled with wonder/intrigued *offer:* supply/provide *extending:* stretching/going from *hardly:* scarcely/barely *account for:* give a reason for/explain *ranks:* lines/rows	Maximum 5
8	The statues ringed the island's shores, but they all had their backs to the sea.	2

Unit 4
Summary Writing

Introduction

Whichever of the Cambridge International Language Examinations you take, you will be asked to write a summary. In this part of the book, we will be looking at the summary question and what skills it tests.

In summary writing you are asked to condense a selected area of text, reproducing facts and ideas that follow the direction of the question, using your own words as far as possible in a piece of well-constructed continuous prose.

You will be given the opportunity to examine all good summary writing skills slowly and gradually.

A summary is marked under two categories:

❶ A mark is given for *content*, that is, the facts that you were asked to select from the passage.

❷ A mark is given for *style*, that is, the accuracy and quality of your writing and the extent to which you are able to use your own words.

As a general rule, the amount of text to be summarised is about 700–800 words, and you will have to summarise it to about one fifth of its original size. You will be given the opening ten words.

A quick deduction will tell you that copying out the first 150 words or so will produce a piece of writing which is of the required length, but which is not a summary. It is clear that good summary writing is about being able to select *key points* from the original text. You must learn how to select these key points and, like other examination skills, this comes through practice.

The chapters that follow will give you practice in selection of *content points*. In later chapters we will move on to *style*.

2 Selection of content points and importance of key instruction words

Here is a reprint of a recent passage set for summary. It is about tourism and its effects on society. The actual question that was set follows on page 226.

❶ If modern holidaymakers have benefited so much
from the growth of the tourist industry, what of the
countries that attract tourists in the first place? On the
face of it, local people are sharing the new-found
wealth of the foreign visitor. Where once there were   5
only undeveloped stretches of coastline, hotels have
sprung up, creating employment for the local
population. The visitors, with money to spend,
encourage business, in particular the restaurant trade,
while craftsmen can find a ready, though seasonal,   10
market for their products. Whereas the local people
once had to work hard on the land or at sea to earn a
slender wage, tourism now provides a more
substantial income.

❷ One might expect that the ever-growing demands of   15
the tourist trade would bring nothing but good for the
countries that receive the holidaymakers. Indeed, a
rosy picture is painted for the long-term future of the
holiday industry. Every month sees the building of a
new hotel somewhere, and every month another rock-   20
bound Pacific island is advertised as the 'last paradise
on earth'. All this means more jobs for yet more
people.

❸ However, the scale and speed of this growth seem set to
destroy the very things tourists want to enjoy. In those   25
countries where there was a rush to make quick money out
of seaside holidays, overcrowded beaches and the concrete
jungles of endless hotels have begun to lose their appeal.
Besides, the holiday towns cannot support the massive influx
of visitors. Sewage spills untreated into the sea and this soon   30
becomes known; visitors begin to look elsewhere for safer
beaches and safer waters to swim in. Nor are the seaside
resorts the only places to suffer from the stranglehold of
tourism. Such is the magical appeal of winter sports for
tourists that hundreds of square kilometres of forests in the   35
mountains of Austria and Switzerland have been destroyed
to make way for hotels, roads, ski lifts and ski runs. But a
series of mild winters and frequent rain has seen severe
flooding and caused landslides; the trees that would have
kept the earth intact are no longer there.   40

❹ Those countries with little experience of tourism can suffer
most. In recent years, Nepal set out to attract foreign visitors
to fund developments in health and education. Its mountains
and valleys, its forests full of wildlife and rare flowers, were
offered to tourists as one more untouched paradise. In fact,   45
the landscape all too soon felt the effects of thousands of
holidaymakers trekking through the forest land. Ancient trails
became major routes for the walkers, with the consequent
destruction of precious trees and plants. One area of Nepal
is invaded by 36 000 walkers a year and their demands for   50
daily provisions and accommodation have quickly outstripped
the natural resources of the countryside and its inhabitants.
Nor have these inhabitants benefited financially from the
tourists. Only a small amount of the visitors' money comes
their way, since the bulk of what the tourists spend is on   55
goods and food imported from outside Nepal.

❺ Not only the environment suffers from the sudden growth of
   tourism. The people rapidly feel its effects as well. Farmland
   makes way for hotels, roads and airports; the old way of life
   goes. If earning a living from the soil was hard, at least it   60
   gave a man independence. Also, the higher wages that can
   be earned in the new luxury hotels have to be paid for. The
   one-time farmer is now the servant of some multinational
   organisation; he is no longer his own master. And he must
   smile at all times. Once it was his back that took the strain;   65
   now it is his smile that is exploited. No doubt he wonders
   whether he wasn't happier in his village working his own plot
   of land.

Note that here, as elsewhere in Unit 4, we are dealing only with the
area to be summarised in the passage set in the comprehension
paper, not the whole passage itself. This book will isolate for you the
area of text to be summarised. However, in the examination it is
very important that you do this yourself before you begin, according
to the instructions in the question. You might even want to mark off
the area with your pencil so that you are not tempted to stray
beyond the boundaries when you begin to write.

Here is the summary question that was set on the passage on
tourism.

Using your own words as far as possible, and using the information
provided in the passage, summarise not only the benefits tourism
can bring, but also the disadvantages.

Your summary, which must be in continuous writing (*not note
form*), must not be longer than 160 words, including the opening
10 words given below.

Begin your summary as follows:

Countries benefit from the growth of tourism, for local people…

Golden rule

You must pay close attention to the instructions given, and follow them, if you are to write a good summary.

So what are the instructions, or *rubric*, as it is more properly called?

- Keep to the word limit allowed.
- Use only the area of text allowed.
- Use the opening 10 words provided.
- Write in continuous prose.
- Summarise the benefits and disadvantages of tourism.

Golden rule

Read the rubric carefully to isolate the *key instruction words*. These tell you what you have to summarise. Keep them in mind as you write your summary. Otherwise, there is a danger that your answer will become irrelevant.

Content points

You will now be given an opportunity to break down this passage about tourism to select content points. The opening 10 words are given to you as a help, not a hindrance. They are specially constructed to lead you into the first point.

You will be awarded 1 mark for every content point that you successfully make. There are always more points available than you would need to find to score full marks.

Now look at the first paragraph in the area designated to be summarised. Refresh your memory about what we call the key instruction words. You will never write a good summary if you lose sight of what you are being asked to do. In this case, the key instruction words are 'benefits' and 'disadvantages'.

If modern holidaymakers have benefited so much from the growth of the tourist industry, what of the countries that attract tourists in the first place? On the face of it, local people are sharing the new-found wealth of the foreign visitor. Where once there were only undeveloped stretches of coastline, hotels have sprung up, creating employment for the local population. The visitors, with money to spend, encourage business, in particular the restaurant trade, while craftsmen can find a ready, though seasonal, market for their products. Whereas the local people once had to work hard on the land or at sea to earn a slender wage, tourism now provides a more substantial income.

Write down what you think are the benefits and disadvantages of tourism listed in the paragraph. At this stage, don't even think about trying to do this in your own words. Think only about the original text wording at this stage.

You should end up with something like this:

1. Local people share the new-found wealth of the foreign visitor.
2. Hotels have sprung up, creating employment for the local population.
3. Visitors with money to spend encourage business.
4. Restaurants and craftsmen benefit particularly.
5. Tourism now provides a more substantial income (than before).

These are all the benefits. You have now reduced the paragraph from 113 to 41 words. They could be set in five consecutive simple sentences and you would score 5 marks for content. Well done!

However, another look will show you that these 41 words can be reduced even further.

For point 1 you could:

- remove 'new-found'
- condense 'wealth of the foreign visitor' into 'foreign visitor's wealth'
- write 'tourist' instead of 'foreign visitor'

For point 2 you could:

- substitute 'new' for the idea of 'have sprung up'
- write 'for locals' instead of 'for the local population'

For point 3 you could:

- substitute 'visitors' expenditure' for 'visitors with money to spend'

For point 4 you could:

- link 'restaurants and craftsmen' to the businesses mentioned in the previous point

For point 5 you could:

- condense 'more substantial' into 'better'

Look at what you now have:

> Local people share tourists' wealth. New hotels create employment for locals. Visitors' expenditure encourages business, particularly for restaurants and craftsmen. Tourism provides a better income.

Now you have scored 5 marks by using only 25 words. At the moment the summary is four simple sentences. There are ways of improving the style of the writing, but, remember, you are concentrating only on content at this stage.

3 Distractors, topic sentences and elaboration points

Here is the second paragraph of the area of text to be summarised.

> One might expect that the ever-growing demands of the tourist trade would bring nothing but good for the countries that receive the holidaymakers. Indeed, a rosy picture is painted for the long-term future of the holiday industry. Every month sees the building of a new hotel somewhere, and every month another rock-bound Pacific island is advertised as the 'last paradise on earth'. All this means more jobs for yet more people.

Distractors

At this stage, it might be a good idea to think about *distractors*. These are phrases or whole sentences, or even groups of sentences, which are irrelevant, not to the sense of the passage, but to the rubric. Remember, you must never lose sight of the task you were given in summary writing, or indeed in any examination. In this case the instructions related to the benefits and disadvantages of tourism.

Look at the first two sentences of the paragraph under consideration. They are a distractor. They do not make any points about benefits or disadvantages of tourism; they merely reiterate that benefits can be expected. However, the third and fourth sentences specify more benefits, again related to hotels and employment.

When summarising these 'benefits' bear in mind the earlier references to hotels and employment, and make sure you differentiate between them. Write down the two content points in the paragraph under consideration. You should have something like this:

> A new hotel is built every month. These create more jobs.

You have scored 2 marks with 11 words.

You might link the ideas like this:

> A new hotel is built every month, creating more jobs.

Now you have 10 words.

You might use the plural form of 'hotel' instead of the singular form, like this:

> New hotels are built every month, creating more jobs.

Now you have 9 words.

You might substitute 'constantly' for 'every month' and substitute 'employment' for 'more jobs'.

> New hotels are constantly built, creating employment.

Now you have 7 words. The original paragraph was 71 words.
Easy, isn't it?

Now have a look at the third paragraph to be summarised.

> However, the scale and speed of this growth seem set to destroy the very things tourists want to enjoy. In those countries where there was a rush to make quick money out of seaside holidays, overcrowded beaches and the concrete jungles of endless hotels have begun to lose their appeal. Besides, the holiday towns cannot

support the massive influx of visitors. Sewage spills untreated into the sea and this soon becomes known; visitors begin to look elsewhere for safer beaches and safer waters to swim in. Nor are the seaside resorts the only places to suffer from the stranglehold of tourism. Such is the magical appeal of winter sports for tourists that hundreds of square kilometres of forests in the mountains of Austria and Switzerland have been destroyed to make way for hotels, roads, ski lifts and ski runs. But a series of mild winters and frequent rain has seen severe flooding and caused landslides; the trees that would have kept the earth intact are no longer there.

Topic sentences

Now let us look at the idea of *topic sentences*. A topic sentence is one which highlights the points which will be, or have been, made in the rest of the paragraph.

Golden rule

A topic sentence is a warning to keep alert.

The first sentence of the paragraph under consideration is the topic sentence. This means we can expect it to herald several points which the writer wishes to make, rather than make any points itself.

The topic sentence we are now looking at is interesting in that it begins with the word 'however'. 'However' is a linking device. Linking devices show either a continuation of ideas or a change of direction. 'However' fits the latter category, that is, it indicates a change of direction of ideas.

So why is all this important? The answer is linked to the key instruction words, which were 'benefits' and 'disadvantages'. In this particular summary you were instructed to write about both.

You have already found several benefits. The linking device, 'however', indicating as it does a change of direction of ideas, should alert you to disadvantages.

To sum up what you have noticed about the third paragraph so far:

- It begins with a topic sentence. You now expect the general point in the topic sentence to be elaborated upon in the remainder of the paragraph.
- It also begins with a linking device. This indicates a change of direction of ideas, so you expect the points to be elaborated to be disadvantages rather than benefits.

Practice session

Write down the disadvantages of tourism mentioned in the paragraph for consideration. Don't worry about 'own words' at this stage.

You should come up with something like this:

1. There are overcrowded beaches.
2. The concrete jungles of endless hotels lose their appeal.
3. Holiday towns cannot support the massive influx of visitors.
4. Sewage spills untreated into the sea.
5. Hundreds of square kilometres of forest in Austria and Switzerland have been destroyed to make way for winter sports for tourists.
6. This destruction has caused landslides.

Elaboration points

Now it is time to think about *elaboration points*. This is a term you will already be familiar with, as it was also used in directed writing.

Elaboration points are ideas, phrases, sentences or even groups of sentences which do not form points in themselves, but give extra information as examples or explanation of ideas. They make language more colourful and varied, but they do not belong in summary writing.

Golden rule

Elaboration points should not be included in your summary.

There are two examples of elaboration points in this paragraph. See if you can identify them.

You should have something like this:

> Visitors begin to look elsewhere for safer beaches and safer waters to swim in. The trees that would have kept the earth intact are no longer there.

These are not disadvantages of tourism; they merely explain the consequence of the fact that sewage spills untreated into the sea and why landslides are bound to happen.

Now read this sentence in the paragraph under consideration again: 'Nor are the seaside resorts the only places to suffer from the stranglehold of tourism.' This might be described as a mini topic sentence, which also changes the direction of the text from beaches to winter sports. It brings about the change of direction by the introductory word 'nor'.

Well done! You may not realise it, but you have now thoroughly analysed this paragraph. You have been helped to pick out the content points (in this case the disadvantages of tourism) by isolating the material unlikely to be making relevant points, namely the topic sentences and the elaboration points.

Practice session

Take a close look at any work of fiction or non-fiction you are currently reading, or even at a good quality newspaper. In any fairly long paragraph, isolate topic sentences and elaboration points. This should leave you with the content of the writer's argument, narrative or newspaper story.

Make this task an ongoing one. You will probably be frustrated to start with, but you might be surprised at how adept you become at this kind of analysis of written material.

Before you leave the paragraph you have been working on, go back to the six content points you found in it and try to rewrite them more concisely. Here they are again:

1. There are overcrowded beaches.
2. The concrete jungles of endless hotels lose their appeal.
3. Holiday towns cannot support the massive influx of visitors.
4. Sewage spills untreated into the sea.
5. Hundreds of square kilometres of forest in Austria and Switzerland have been destroyed to make way for winter sports for tourists.
6. This destruction has caused landslides.

Use the summary of Para 1 in Chapter 2 to help you. Again, don't worry about using your own words. You might have something like this:

> There are overcrowded beaches and concrete jungles of endless hotels. Holiday towns cannot support all the visitors, and sewage spills untreated into the sea. Large areas of forest in Austria and Switzerland have been destroyed for winter sports, causing landslides.

Well done! You have scored 6 marks for content by using only 40 words. In the next chapter we will have a look at the fourth paragraph to be summarised.

Content points — linking devices

Here is the fourth paragraph we need to summarise:

> Those countries with little experience of tourism can suffer most. In recent years, Nepal set out to attract foreign visitors to fund developments in health and education. Its mountains and valleys, its forests full of wildlife and rare flowers, were offered to tourists as one more untouched paradise. In fact, the landscape all too soon felt the effects of thousands of holidaymakers trekking through the forest land. Ancient trails became major routes for the walkers, with the consequent destruction of precious trees and plants. One area of Nepal is invaded by 36 000 walkers a year and their demands for daily provisions and accommodation have quickly outstripped the natural resources of the countryside and its inhabitants. Nor have these inhabitants benefited financially from the tourists. Only a small amount of the visitors' money comes their way, since the bulk of what the tourists spend is on goods and food imported from outside Nepal.

A careful reading of the paragraph tells you that it is about the effects of tourism on Nepal. It is always worthwhile to come back to the rubric, i.e. what you were instructed to do. In this case, benefits and disadvantages of tourism should be in the forefront of your mind.

Golden rule

Always keep the rubric in mind.

The first sentence is a topic sentence, heralding 'disadvantages' by the word 'suffer'. You would be right to dismiss the next two sentences as distractors. They tell you nothing about disadvantages.

236

As you move on to the sentence beginning, 'In fact, the landscape...', notice that the disadvantages begin.

Write down the disadvantages of tourism mentioned in this paragraph under consideration. You should find four disadvantages as follows:

1. Thousands of holidaymakers trek through the forest land of Nepal.
2. Precious trees and plants are destroyed.
3. The inhabitants of Nepal do not benefit financially.
4. Tourists spend their money on goods and food imported from outside Nepal.

In selecting the disadvantages from the text you may hesitate over the sentence beginning, 'One area of Nepal'. This sentence tells you that one area of Nepal does not have enough provisions and accommodation for the tourists. However, it is not a disadvantage of tourism, but a consequence of it. It is therefore an elaboration point.

Practice session

Write down the four content points given above, combining them in a single paragraph. Try to make your paragraph as concise as possible. Don't worry about using your own words at this stage.

You might end up with something like this:

Thousands of tourists trek through the forests of Nepal, destroying precious trees and plants. Local people do not benefit financially, because tourists buy imported, not local, goods and food.

Thus you pick up the 4 marks in 29 words.

Look now at the word 'destroying' in the previous paragraph. This part of the verb, ending in -ing, is the *present participle*. It is a useful device to use in summary writing because it achieves two things.

- Firstly, it can be used to reduce the number of words needed to form the verb. In this case 'and precious trees... are destroyed' comes down to 'destroying precious trees...'
- Secondly, the present participle is useful for linking content points.

At the moment you are thinking only of *content*, but later you will also be thinking about *style*. Linking is a feature of good style and you will be credited for your ability to use good linking devices.

Look back on our final versions of Paras 2 and 3 of the present summary (Chapter 3). Each of these contains a present participle used as a linking device:

- In our version of Para 2 we wrote '... creating employment.'

- In our version of Para 3 we wrote '... causing landslides.'

Now we come to the last paragraph to be summarised from the passage on tourism. The paragraph contains nine sentences. By now you should feel more confident about analysing a paragraph for topic sentences, distractors and content points.

Not only the environment can suffer from the sudden growth of tourism. The people rapidly feel its effects as well. Farmland makes way for hotels, roads and airports; the old way of life goes. If earning a living from the soil was hard, at least it gave a man independence. Also, the higher wages that can be earned in the new luxury hotels have to be paid for. The one-time farmer is now the servant of some multinational organisation; he is no longer his own master. And he must smile at all times. Once it was his back that took the strain; now it is his smile that is exploited. No doubt he wonders whether he wasn't happier in his village working his own plot of land.

How does this paragraph shape up? Examine it as we have done the others and write down your results.

You should get something like this:

- Sentence 1: *Topic sentence*
  The word 'suffer' indicates one of the key instruction words from the rubric, i.e. 'disadvantages'. But there's nothing to write down yet.

- Sentence 2: *Elaboration point*
  The sentence merely extends the idea of Sentence 1.

- Sentence 3: *Content points numbers 1 and 2*
  - Farmland makes way for hotels, roads and airports.
  - The old way of life has gone.

- Sentence 4: *Elaboration point*
  The sentence reflects on the contents of the previous sentence. It tells you two things about the farmer's way of life: he worked hard and he was independent. However, it tells you nothing whatsoever about the benefits and disadvantages of tourism.

Now you can locate the remaining points in the paragraph, as follows:

- Sentence 5: *Content point number 3*
  This sentence makes the point that people who used to be farmers earn more through tourism. This is not the same as the point made about higher wages in Para 1 of your summary. Here the emphasis is on one-time farmers.

This point is difficult to spot if you lose sight of the rubric. You should not have become so locked into 'disadvantages' by this time that you forget about 'benefits'.

- Sentence 6: *Content point number 4*
  The farmer is no longer his own master.

- Sentences 7, 8 and 9: *Content point number 5*
  Here the writer is making the general point that the farmer's good nature is being exploited. He is earning more money, but he has lost his independence and must please his employer rather than himself.

This condenses into content point number five: the farmer has to be obedient (or submissive). But it could not have been made by merely lifting from the text. It involves making a general point from a particular example.

At first sight, you may have dismissed these sentences as distractors. If you did, don't worry! There are more content points in any text to be summarised than the number you are required to find to score full marks. You don't have to find them all.

So now your summary of the paragraph might look like this:

> Farmland makes way for hotels. The old way of life goes. The farmer earns more money. He is no longer independent. He has to be obedient to his employer.

You have now reduced the original paragraph of 128 words to 29 words. However, you might not be happy about the one benefit of tourism being among the four disadvantages. You might also be unhappy about the rather staccato sound of these five simple sentences.

If you are unhappy about one of these problems, good for you! If you are unhappy about both of them, even better! It shows that your summary writing skills are improving already.

Practice session

> Combine these five sentences to produce a more fluent
> paragraph. The one benefit of tourism already mentioned should
> sit comfortably alongside the four disadvantages mentioned.

You might have something like this:

> Farmland makes way for hotels, consequently destroying the old way
> of life. Although the farmer earns more, he is no longer his own
> master, and needs to obey his employer.

Note the following words used:

- 'destroying'. This is a present participle, linking two content
  points.
- 'consequently'. This is a linking device, adding fluency to the
  sentence.
- 'although'. This shows a change in direction. (Look again at
  page 232.) Thus, the 'benefit' can sit comfortably alongside the
  contrasting 'disadvantages'.

Now the complete summary can be set out. The simple sentences of
the opening sections have been combined to make a more fluent
piece of writing. Also the opening ten words provided in the rubric
have been included.

The completed summary could look like this:

> Countries benefit from the growth of tourism, for local people share the wealth of tourists. New hotels create employment, while visitors' expenditure encourages business, particularly among restaurants and craftsmen. Tourism provides a better income. New hotels are constantly being built, creating even more jobs. However, disadvantages include overcrowded beaches and concrete jungles of endless hotels. Holiday towns cannot support all the visitors, and sewage spills untreated into the sea. Large areas of forest in Austria and Switzerland have been destroyed for winter sports, causing landslides. Thousands of tourists trek through the forests of Nepal, destroying precious trees and plants. Local people do not benefit financially because tourists buy imported, not local, goods and food. Farmland makes way for hotels, consequently destroying the old way of life. Although the farmer earns more, he is no longer his own master, and needs to obey his employer.
>
> (144 words)

The original text has been summarised in 144 words, including the ten opening words given in the rubric.

You haven't been worried at this point about writing in your own words. But we have tried to keep words used to a minimum. So how can you do this? Here are some rules to follow.

❶ Link content points using a present participle when possible, e.g. 'Hotels opened, creating employment.'

❷ Use pronouns wherever possible without obscuring the sense, e.g. 'he' instead of 'the author'; 'they' instead of 'the tourists'.

❸ Don't use topic sentences, even if the original text uses them. Don't say, for example, 'There were many disadvantages brought about by tourism.' Just get straight on to writing down the disadvantages.

❹ Don't think that contracting words will save words. It won't. Two words contracted into one still count as two words. In any case, contracted words have no place in the formal language of summary writing.

In completing the first stage of the summary question, we have been concentrating on content points. In the next chapters we will consider the element that also contributes towards successful summary writing, which is style. This is the extent to which you are able to use your own words as far as possible in a piece of well-constructed continuous prose. See Chapter 1.

5

Style – use of own words

Your final summary will be assessed under two headings. These are content and style.

You have now learned a lot about the assessment of content, and have developed strategies to ensure that you make as many content points as possible.

Now is the time to look at style. There are 10 marks allocated to the style in which your summary is written.

First of all, what is meant by style? Write a sentence or two in your notebook to define the features you think a 'stylish' piece of summary writing should have. Use your knowledge of continuous writing from earlier in this book to help you. It would not be cheating – in fact it would be quite sensible.

Although good summary writing contains many of the features of good continuous writing, 'imagination' is not one of them. Summary writing should combine stylistic features within a *factually* written context.

Marking criteria

Basically, examiners judge the style of a piece of summary writing under two categories. These are:

❶ Use of own words

❷ Use of English

Golden rule

The more you manage to avoid the original wording the higher your mark for own words will be.

Consider the following section of text. It comes from a passage about Man's relationship with animals.

Passage 1

> In some parts of Europe, special parks called safari parks have been set up. Here, small herds of game and troops of monkeys can move about freely, although serious drawbacks have emerged. Some of these animals are made ill by exhaust fumes from visitors' cars, and tropical animals, which do not belong in Europe's northern climate, may suffer through not having suitable winter quarters. For all their faults, zoos and safari parks are a lifeline to nature, a slender thread that leads us to an increasing interest in living things.

The rubric for the summary question on the passage asked candidates to select ways in which Man has mistreated and misrepresented animals.

In this part of the text, therefore, two content points can be seen. They are:

- Some of the animals in safari parks are made ill by fumes from visitors' cars.
- Tropical animals which do not belong in Europe's northern climate may suffer through not having suitable winter quarters.

Now consider the work of four candidates on this part of the text.

Example 1 – Complete transcript
Candidate A summarised the section of text by lifting all of it, word for word. She gained two marks for content points but is not entitled to any marks whatsoever for use of own words.

This type of writing is called a complete transcript of the original text and should clearly be avoided. Another obvious disadvantage of a complete transcript, apart from its effects on the style mark, is that it uses up the allotted number of words very quickly. This in turn affects the content mark; the candidate runs out of words before amassing enough points.

This particular transcript uses up 90 words – the whole of the paragraph in effect – and makes only two content points.

Example 2 – Wholesale copying
Candidate B summarised the text in this way:

> In safari parks, some animals are made ill by exhaust fumes, and tropical animals, which do not belong in Europe's northern climate, may suffer through not having suitable winter quarters.

Candidate B has obviously done a better job than Candidate A. Firstly, she has avoided the topic sentence. This reads, 'In some parts of Europe, special parks called safari parks have been set up.' (This is not a content point in itself.)

Secondly, she has avoided the elaboration point. This reads, 'Here, small herds of game and troops of monkeys can move about freely.' Thirdly, she has also avoided the distractor. This reads, 'For all their faults, zoos and safari parks are a lifeline to nature, a slender thread that leads us to an increasing interest in living things.' In addition, she has carefully filtered out the two content points.

Notice, too, another positive point about this summary. The candidate has neatly transferred 'safari parks' from one part of the text to another.

However, she has lifted the text to make the content points. This type of writing often avoids the irrelevant sections of the text such as topic sentences, distractors and elaboration points. Nevertheless, because it makes no attempt to use the candidate's own words, it is called wholesale copying.

All the same, it is much better than a complete transcript. It cuts down considerably on the number of words used, and so allows more content points to be made. However, it would gain no credit in the use of own words category.

Is it possible to produce a better piece of summary writing in your own words?

Summarise the two content points from this text using your own words as far as possible.

Example 3 – Using own words
Now look at Candidate C's version: Ask yourself whether your version is better or worse than this.

> Animals in safari parks are sick because of exhaust fumes from tourists' cars, and animals from the tropics suffer in Europe's northern climate because they do not have appropriate living quarters for winter.

Write down ways in which this version is better than those of Candidate B and Candidate A. (If you don't think it is better, go back to the start of the chapter!)

Example 4 – Using own words well
Finally, here is the work of Candidate D:

> Pollution from the exhausts of tourists' cars causes sickness among safari park animals, and some of them coming from hot countries are unable to adapt to cold winters and also suffer.

Because this candidate has made a sustained attempt to use her own words, and has done so successfully, she will score a high mark for use of own words.

Note about using own words
When you are asked to use your own words, it does not mean that all the words in the passage have to be substituted. The introduction to the comprehension paper requires you to:

> Summarise a selected area of text, reproducing facts and ideas that follow the direction of the question, using your own words *as far as possible* in a piece of well-constructed continuous prose.

Note the wording 'as far as possible'. This means you do not have to substitute all the words.

Candidates A, B, C and D were therefore not expected to avoid words like 'animals', 'tourists' and 'safari'. What you must do in the use of own words is to avoid lifting entire lines or whole stretches of text. The extent to which you are able to do this will determine your final mark for use of own words, and consequently your overall mark for style.

Golden rule

Avoid lifting lines or whole stretches of the text. Use your own words as far as possible.

Here is another section for summary from the passage about Man and animals. The rubric for the summary task remains the same as for the last section you considered, namely to select the ways in which Man has mistreated and misrepresented animals, using your own words as far as possible.

Passage 2

Before the advent of the cinema and television, city-dwellers rarely encountered wild animals in any form except in zoos. Even when the cinema arrived, the impression of animals it gave was not helpful. Animals were depicted in early films as savage killers, attacking the hero, or being gunned down by brave hunters in the name of sport. It was not until the invention of colour television in the late 1960s that many magnificent natural history films were made which provided an awareness of what wild animals are really like by showing them in their natural surroundings. Animals also suffered at the hands of Man in that they were gradually but systematically destroyed by Europeans to make way for agricultural land to provide food for a fast-growing population.

Summarise this section of the text. Find the two content points and express them in your own words.

Your summary should read something like this:

> Films showed animals as bloodthirsty killers. The need for
> agricultural land meant that animals had to be killed.

A complete transcript would have scored 2 marks for content, but
nothing whatsoever for use of own words. It would have wasted
valuable words by using all 127 words of the section to make only 2
marks.

Wholesale copying would have edited the text by avoiding
distractors, elaboration points and topic sentences.

It would have read something like this:

> When the cinema arrived, animals were depicted as savage killers,
> attacking the hero. Animals also suffered at the hands of Man in that
> they were gradually destroyed to make way for agricultural land to
> provide food.

This example of wholesale copying uses 36 words and scores 2
marks for content. However, it would score few marks for use of
own words.

Here is another section from the same text about Man and animals.

Passage 3

> Today, however, the wild animals of Africa, like their European
> counterparts in safari parks, are more likely to suffer from exhaust
> fumes than gunshot wounds. Tourist pollution is considered the
> main cause in the dramatic decline of the numbers of certain
> predatory animals like the cheetah and leopard. In desperation,
> some of these animals have abandoned their natural behaviour
> patterns and concentrate on nocturnal hunting to avoid the swarm
> of trucks, zebra-striped vans and other vehicles that bump and lurch
> through the game parks from first light.

Practice session

> Examine this section of the text about Man and animals. It
> contains three content points. Pick out these three points and
> express them in your own words.

Your summary should read like this:

> In Africa, animals that are predators are dying off because of tourist
> pollution. They are forced to give up their normal way of life and
> have to hunt at night.

Well done! You have 3 marks for content and a high mark for use of
own words. Also, you have reduced the words from 87 in the
original section of text to 30 words.

6

Style – use of English

You may think that the term 'use of English' seems, at first glance, either a very vague one, or one which is so broad you don't even know where to begin. Don't worry!

In this chapter, we will break down the term 'use of English' into something more understandable and meaningful.

Examiners think of use of English under three headings:

❶ Mechanical accuracy

❷ Sentence structure

❸ Organisation and linking

Mechanical accuracy

This means the ability to write without making errors of grammar, spelling or punctuation.

List in your notebook what you think are the most serious errors which can be made in any type of writing. You should come up with something like this:

- Wrong verb forms, e.g., 'Safari parks had being set up'
- Serious tense errors, e.g., 'Animals suffer and died'
- Omission or misuse of prepositions, e.g., 'Animals do not belong Europe's climate'; 'animals on safari parks'
- Serious errors of sentence structure, e.g., 'Tropical animals, unable to adapt to cold climates, and die'
- Errors of agreement, e.g., 'New hotels creates employment'

Although you will not earn a poor mark for style just because you made errors, it is best to make as few errors as possible. Examiners will not penalise a minor spelling slip, provided it does not seriously distort the meaning.

Similarly, don't worry about long lists of 'examination offences' you might have seen. The emphasis of assessment in style is on what you can do, not on what you cannot do.

Look at any piece of work you have completed recently and had marked or corrected by your teacher. It can be any type of writing – continuous, directed or summary. Make three columns in your notebook. In column one, write down any errors you have made. In column two, write down the corrected version. In column three, write down the type of error it is.

You might end up with something like this:

Column one	Column two	Column three
Many collection of skull	Many collections of skulls	Plural endings
Curiosity of animal life	Curiosity about animal life	Prepositions
Farmers use pesticides and made animals suffer	Farmers used pesticides and made animals suffer	Formation of past tenses

Golden rule

Isolate your main errors. Try to improve step by step. Read through your work to check for errors.

Now you have isolated the types of errors you seem prone to make. They suggest you should revise:

- agreements, i.e. the distinction between plural and singular nouns
- prepositions
- verb formations, especially tenses

Sentence structure

One of the things you will be assessed for in summary writing is your ability to write in sentences and to vary their types.

Read the following section to be summarised. There are three marks for content in this section.

> Animals came to be used for entertainment, often of a degrading nature. Travelling showmen included performing monkeys and dancing bears in their displays, making these animals look foolish. Circuses attracted crowds curious to see animals specially trained to entertain them with their tricks. Audiences felt a satisfying glow of superiority as they witnessed their antics, insensitive to the humiliation the creatures suffered.

Now look at the work of Candidates A, B and C. The rubric provided them with 10 opening words to take them into the summary, as follows:

'In relatively recent times, Man mistreated animals, using them for...'

Example 1
Candidate A wrote:

> In relatively recent times, Man mistreated animals, using them for entertainment. He made animals look foolish. He also humiliated them.

He scores 3 marks for content. Without worrying about the use of own words, what do you notice about the sentence structure?

He has basically written simple sentences. His use of 'using' was given to him in the rubric. He will not score well for style under the heading of sentence structure if his whole summary is written like this.

Write down your own version of these sentences, combining them into a complex sentence. How did you get on? How is it possible to create a complex sentence from a run of simple sentences?

Here are three ways:

❶ Use conjunctions, e.g. words like 'and', 'but', 'since' and 'when'.

❷ Use present participles, i.e. the part of the verb ending in -ing.

❸ Use relative pronouns, i.e. 'who', 'whose', 'whom', 'which' and 'that'.

Example 2
Now look at the work of Candidate B. See if you can work out the methods he used to make one complex sentence.

> In relatively recent times, Man mistreated animals, using them for entertainment, which made them look foolish and humiliated them.

You will have seen that the candidate used a relative pronoun ('which') and a conjunction ('and'). The present participle 'using' was provided in the 10 opening words.

Example 3
Finally, look at the work of Candidate C. What methods did he use to make the following complex sentence?

> In relatively recent times, Man mistreated animals, using them for entertainment, making them look foolish and humiliating them.

This candidate has used two present participles of his own ('making' and 'humiliating') and a conjunction ('and') to make a complex sentence out of three simple sentences. Note that 'using' was provided in the 10 opening words.

All three candidates managed to avoid elaboration points about 'travelling showmen', 'bears' and 'monkeys' and the sentence about 'circuses'. They also avoided the distractor in the text – the reference to audiences feeling a 'satisfying glow of superiority'.

Organisation and linking

This is the last of the three headings which the examiners use to assess your use of English.

Good organisation and linking produce a fluent piece of writing. Your first draft of a summary may be written in sentences, but it is usually rather abrupt or disjointed. This is because you have been concentrating on content, and thought little about style and organising your writing. Your second draft gives you the opportunity to think about organisation.

Though you can generally follow the sequence of the text in selecting points, often you can combine two or three points in one 'unit'. Not only will you save words, you will give the summary a better 'flow'.

Sometimes you can take a point in a later stage of the text and link it to one made earlier, if they belong together naturally. This is not always easy to do. But thinking about it is a step in the right direction. Don't 'scramble' points to get this effect!

Linking is another technique which can give your writing fluency and 'flow'. Words like 'however', 'although' and 'also' are linking devices. They indicate a change of direction in the writing or a continuation of ideas.

Write down some linking devices in your notebook which could indicate a continuation of ideas.

You might have something like this:

'in addition', 'also', 'furthermore', 'moreover'.

Now write down some which could indicate a change of direction.

You might have written:

'however', 'nevertheless', 'on the other hand', 'still', 'but'.

You have now covered the important elements in composing the content of a summary, and in producing good style. Think about all the summary writing skills you have learned and write them down.

❶ You have learnt that it is important to:

- read the rubric properly
- pick out the key instruction words
- check the area of text to be summarised
- keep to the word limit laid down for the summary
- use the opening words provided in the rubric

❷ You have also learnt how to:

- isolate content points and distinguish them from distractors
- identify elaboration points
- identify topic sentences

❸ You have also seen that you should:

- leave enough time to compose a full draft for your summary before composing your finished version
- use your own words as far as possible
- try to use a variety of sentence structures
- bring in linking devices
- check your work for errors

Golden rule

> The more you can combine these skills, the higher your overall mark for summary writing will be.

In the next chapter you will be working on a complete summary question.

Ready to begin?

A complete summary – examples of worked answers

You are now ready to begin work on a complete summary question. Here is the text to be summarised. It is all about the ancient city of Pompeii in Italy, which was totally buried in a volcanic eruption in AD 79.

❶ Through time, Pompeii almost completely slipped from the world's memory. Even among scholars, the precise location of Pompeii remained unknown, primarily because a thick flow of molten rock had poured over the area from eruptions in later years. 5
This had entirely altered the shape of the coast. Also, when the digging to uncover the ruins began in the 18th century, the debris from these excavations had been left in scattered heaps around the site, further obscuring it. Rainwater, too, collected and had 10
hastened its decay. These early excavators had acted for the sake of plunder; they made no genuine effort to investigate the past. This did not come about until the appointment in 1860 of the archaeologist Fiorelli as director of the excavations. 15

❷ Fiorelli set as his goal the total recovery of the vanished city of Pompeii. His approach was the essence of discipline and orderliness. He removed all the debris that had piled up during earlier excavations and installed a drainage system to draw off the 20
rainwater. He differed from previous archaeologists because he was the first to believe that a systematic study of the ruins and all that they contained was essential. Only in this way could their past history be thoroughly understood. After tracing the perimeter 25
walls, he mapped out the site and divided it into districts, identifying individual buildings and carefully numbering them in a logical sequence.

❸ Bit by bit, as details accumulated and were pieced together, the long buried past came alive. Because the city and its   30
houses had been taken from the world almost intact, they could be brought back almost whole. As the work proceeded, Fiorelli made sure that every new object that emerged was given a precise description, not just of its appearance and nature, but also of its position in relation to   35
other objects. He insisted that, whenever possible, new discoveries were left in place rather than removed for shipment to a museum or storehouse. Not only interior wall paintings were left intact, but also exterior notices, shop signs and even graffiti.   40

❹ As he worked, he recorded his progress in journals to help future archaeologists, many of whom followed this lead set by Fiorelli. As a result of his excavations, all manner of household items were found: eggs and fish were discovered lying on a dining table, as well as pots containing meat   45
bones. Personal items of every kind turned up, like jewellery, cosmetics, perfume and combs. In a way, voices could be heard as well, as the graffiti that were uncovered gave insight into the lives of the citizens of Pompeii. Among these scribblings on the walls were messages from lovers, personal   50
attacks and casual observations on the world in general. The excavation told a story of ordinary life stopped in its tracks.

❺ And then there were the people themselves, recovered by a method that even today still seems almost magical…

❻ At Pompeii, volcanic ash had been the cause of a sort of   55
preservation miracle. During the later phases of the eruption, this ash enveloped many of the victims and then solidified around them, leaving body-shaped cavities behind when the flesh decayed. Fiorelli was the first to realise the possibility that there were human remains buried in the ruins of the   60
city, and that their impressions might have been left deep in the sandy covering of volcanic ash.

❼ The moment of discovery occurred in February 1863, when
a workman accidentally made a hole in a mound at the site.
Fiorelli noticed that there was a cavity of some sort. He   65
ordered liquid plaster to be poured into the cavity and given
time to solidify. He had the surrounding ash removed,
revealing a complete figure that was uncannily life-like.
Eventually, he was responsible for many victims being
uncovered by this technique, and people's fascination grew   70
as the intimate details of Pompeii's tragic story were
disclosed. The plaster casts fixed the terror and desperation
of that long ago disaster in a kind of eternal present.

Now here is the summary question set on the text:

In 1860, the archaeologist Fiorelli undertook the task of uncovering
the ruins of Pompeii.

Using your own words as far as possible, write a summary of the
problems he faced when he began his work, what methods he
employed to restore the ancient city accurately, and how he used
the volcanic ash to produce his most amazing discoveries.

Your summary, which must be in continuous writing (*not note
form*), must not be longer than 160 words, including the opening
10 words given below.

Begin your summary as follows:

Over the centuries, people had eventually forgotten about Pompeii
because…

Step 1
Read the question and pick out the key instruction words.
You should have: 'problems', 'methods to restore' and 'used
volcanic ash'.

Step 2

Read the area of text to be summarised, in this case the whole of the passage printed at the beginning of this chapter.

The section for summary was selected from a much wider area of text, not all of which is printed here. But make sure that you identify the area to be summarised in the exam.

Step 3

Pick out the content points. Remember that there will be more points available than the number you need to gain full marks for content.

Here is a list of the content points. Don't look at it until you have tried to find them for yourself!

The list uses the words of the text, for two reasons. Firstly, they make the points easier for you to recognise at this stage. Secondly, that is probably how you would compile your own list to start with.

But remember, credit will be given for the extent to which you use your own words in your final version. Even the substitution of an occasional word is better than nothing.

Your list should look something like this:

	Line No.
Para 1	
1. the location of Pompeii remained unknown	2–3
2. because the molten rock had poured over the area from later eruptions	4–5
3. this had altered the shape of the coast	6
4. debris from excavations had obscured the site	8–10
5. rainwater had hastened the decay of the site	10–11

	Line No.
Para 2	
6. Fiorelli's approach was orderly/disciplined	17–18
7. he removed all the debris	18–19
8. he installed a drainage system	20
9. he made a systematic study of the ruins	22–23
10. he traced the perimeter walls	25–26
11. he mapped out the site/divided it into districts	26–27
12. he identified/numbered the buildings	27–28
Para 3	
13. he gave each object a precise description	33–34
14. and recorded its position	35–36
15. he left discoveries in their positions/did not remove them	37–38
Para 4	
16. he recorded his progress in journals	41
Para 6	
17. he realised that human remains could be found	59–60
Para 7	
18. he noticed there was a cavity/hole	65
19. he ordered liquid plaster to be poured into it	65–66
20. he allowed it to solidify	66–67
21. he had the surrounding ash removed	67
22. and he revealed figures/victims	68

Step 4

Go back through the text and pick out any distractors, elaboration points or topic sentences you can find.

You should have something like this:

			Line No.
Para 1			
1. 'These early excavators… as director of the excavations'	*distractor*		11–15
Para 2			
2. 'Fiorelli set as his goal the total recovery of… Pompeii.'	*topic sentence*		16–17
3. 'He differed from previous archaeologists'	*distractor*		21
4. 'Only in this way could their past history be… understood'	*elaboration point*		24–25
Para 3			
5. 'Bit by bit… brought back almost whole.'	*topic sentences*		29–32
6. 'Not only interior wall paintings were left intact… even graffiti.'	*elaboration point*		38–40
Para 4			
7. 'As a result of his excavations…' to the end of the paragraph.	*distractor*		43–52
Para 5			
8. This short paragraph is a *topic sentence* or, more exactly, a *topic paragraph*.			53–54

		Line No.
Para 6		
9. 'At Pompeii, volcanic ash had been the cause of a sort of preservation miracle… leaving body-shaped cavities behind when the flesh decayed.'	*elaboration points*	55–59
Para 7		
10. 'The moment of discovery occurred… when a workman accidentally made a hole in a mound at the site.'	*elaboration point*	63–64
11. 'and people's fascination grew as the intimate details of Pompeii's tragic story were disclosed. The plaster casts fixed the terror and desperation of that long ago disaster in a kind of eternal present.'	*distractor*	70–73

Now let us look at two sample summaries of the Pompeii passage, one by Candidate A, the other by Candidate B.

In each case the writer has scored 15 marks for the content. That is the maximum mark possible under the content heading on this type of summary. We can therefore go straight on to consider the style of the writing.

To help you recognise the content points, the numbers assigned to them on pages 261–262 of this chapter are inserted in the candidates' writing as the points are made.

Example 1 – Candidate A

Over the centuries, people had eventually forgotten about Pompeii
because its precise location remained unknown (1), because molten
rock had poured over the area from eruptions in later years (2) and
altered the shape of the coast (3). Debris obscured the site (4) and
rainwater hastened its decay (5). Fiorelli's approach was the essence
of discipline and orderliness (6). He removed all the debris (7) and
installed a drainage system to draw off the rainwater (8). He
believed in a systematic study of the ruins (9) and traced the
perimeter walls (10), mapping out the site (11) and numbering
buildings (12). He gave each new object a precise description (13)
and insisted that new discoveries were left in place rather than
removed for shipment to a museum (15). He recorded his progress
in journals (16). He was the first to notice that there might be
human remains buried in the ruins (17). He noticed a cavity (18)
and ordered liquid plaster to be poured into it (19). He had the
surrounding ash removed (21), revealing a complete figure (22).

(159 words)

To his credit, Candidate A has:

- distilled the relevant detail and avoided distractors and
  elaboration points
- accumulated the maximum number of content points allowed
  (15)
- covered the whole area of the text to be summarised

Also, under *mechanical accuracy* of writing, the candidate has made
no errors at all.

However, under the heading of *use of own words*, you will see that
the candidate does little more than copy wholesale from the text,
though there are some attempts to reshape the text, for example:

- 'He *believed* in a systematic study'
- 'and *traced* the perimeter walls'

- '*mapping* out the site and *numbering* buildings'
- 'He *gave* each new object a precise description'
- 'He was the first to realise *that there might be* human remains'

Nevertheless, the candidate has done little – outside these minor changes to the text – to use his own words.

Under the heading of *sentence structure*, the first sentence is a 'complex' one. It has three conjunctions, but it relies heavily on the text, and the word 'because' is awkwardly repeated. The remainder of the writing is in simple sentences, combined here and there with a repetitive use of 'and'.

There is one area of credit, where the candidate uses the present participle to good effect: 'mapping out the site and numbering buildings'. For the most part, however, the candidate relies on simple sentences, linked by the conjunction 'and'.

Under the heading of *organisation and linking*, there are no clear attempts at linking the ideas; in fact, most sentences merely begin with the pronoun 'he', which is repetitive.

Now let us look at Candidate B's summary. The content points have their numbers inserted as recorded on pages 261–262 of this chapter.

Example 2 – Candidate B

> Over the centuries, people had eventually forgotten about Pompeii because its exact position was unclear (1), owing mainly to lava from subsequent eruptions covering the area (2), thus changing the coastline (3). Besides, rubbish from excavations littered the site, hiding it even more (4), while rainwater accelerated its decay (5). Using a disciplined approach (6) and believing in a methodical study (9), Fiorelli cleared the rubbish (7), putting in a drainage system (8). Furthermore, his tactics included locating the outside walls (10), producing maps of the site (11), splitting it into areas and establishing the identity of particular buildings (12). He ensured that new discoveries were given exact descriptions (13), and left where they were rather than removed (15). He also noted his discoveries in journals (16). He realised that humans might be buried in the city (17), and so, when he spotted a cavity in some earth (18), he had liquid plaster put into it (19), and allowed it to set (20). When the surrounding ash was taken away (21), a human figure was seen (22).   (156 words)

Like Candidate A, Candidate B has:

- distilled the relevant detail and avoided distractors and elaboration points
- accumulated the maximum number of content points allowed (15)
- covered the whole area of the text to be summarised

Also, under *mechanical accuracy*, Candidate B has made no errors at all.

Under the heading of *use of own words*, Candidate B has made a sustained and successful attempt to use his own words, in contrast to the heavy 'lifting' used by Candidate A. Note just some of the effective substitutions Candidate B has made:

Text wording	Line ref. in text	Candidate's wording
'precise location remained unknown'	3	'exact position was unclear'
'primarily because'	4	'owing mainly to'
'in later years'	5	'subsequent'
'altered the shape of the coast'	6	'changing the coastline'
'obscuring'	10	'hiding'
'hastened'	11	'accelerated'
'tracing the perimeter walls'	25–26	'locating the outside walls'
'were left in place'	37	'left where they were'

Under the heading of *sentence structure*, this candidate constructs some complex sentences, using the following features.

❶ Present participles

- 'covering the area'
- 'changing the coastline'
- 'hiding it even more'
- 'putting in a drainage system'

Often the present participle allows the candidate to economise on the original wording.

What other examples of present participles can you find in the candidate's writing?

❷ Conjunctions

The use of conjunctions, e.g. 'and', 'while', 'where' and 'when' enables the candidate to construct sentences 'inside' the main sentence, i.e. subordinate clauses.

Some examples are:

- 'Rubbish littered the site... while rainwater hastened its decay.'
- 'He realised that humans might be buried in the city and so, when he spotted a cavity... he had liquid plaster put into it, and allowed it to set.'

This ability to shape subordinate clauses gives the candidate's writing variety; it also avoids the repetitive use of 'and'.

Under *organisation and linking*, the candidate maintains a good 'flow' to his writing by using the following:

❶ Linking words

- 'thus changing the coastline'
- 'Besides, rubbish from excavations littered the site...'
- 'Furthermore, his tactics included...'
- 'He also noted his discoveries...'

❷ Organisation

The candidate has maintained an orderly sequence of ideas in following the key instruction words of the question. Let's check these instructions again:

- the *problems* Fiorelli faced when he began his work
- the *methods* he employed to restore the ancient city accurately
- how he *used the volcanic ash* to produce his most amazing discoveries

Notice how the candidate has kept these key instruction words of the question rubric in clear focus, avoiding irrelevance. His use of linking words sharpens the focus even further. This candidate will score well in style assessment, that is, for the *use of own words*, and for the *use of English*.

8 Practice summary question

Here is another passage for summary. It is taken from a longer section of text, not all of which is printed here. Summarise the whole of the section printed below.

❶ I had been told previously that I would need a licence to play my violin in the street for money. So off I went after breakfast to the city hall. Soldiers with rifles on their knees sat around on the stairs of the building and dogs were running in and out around them like busy messenger boys. I   5
dodged past them and then was confronted by a motionless queue of peasants waiting for some official or other. Doubting that there would be a queue for violin players like myself, I hurried past them, climbed some stairs and opened the first door that I came to.   10

❷ At a desk by the window sat a city magistrate, his feet on a nearby cabinet, a cigar hanging from his mouth and a chessboard balanced across his knees. He looked as thin as a reed. He was humming quietly to himself, and seemed unaware of my presence; then suddenly he swung his chair   15
round towards me. His face, seen front-on, almost disappeared from view, so unusually thin was his whole appearance. I was aware of two raised eyebrows and an expression of enquiry, but that was all. When I told him what I wanted, he gave a little squeak, and the eyebrows jumped   20
with pleasure. He immediately sat up and began to write. His pen carefully traced a series of delicate characters over the paper in a bright violet ink. He signed it with a flourish. 'There,' he said. 'The city is yours for you and your violin. That will be half a peseta.'   25

❸ Later, armed with my licence, and a brand new straw hat purchased that day in a nearby market, I went back to my lodgings to fetch my violin and get to work. I walked around until I found a busy lane, placed my hat on the ground, and started to play a tune. According to my experience in other   30

271

countries, a few people should have stopped, if only out of
curiosity, and then dropped some money into my hat before
passing on by. But it didn't work out that way here. No
sooner had I started playing than everybody in the lane
dropped what they were doing and crowded round me.   35
They stood in stony silence, blocking the traffic, blotting out
the sun, and treading my new straw hat into the ground.
Again and again I fished it out from under their feet for their
contributions; it remained obstinately empty. Then I moved
on somewhere else. As soon as I started to play again, the   40
crowd re-formed and encircled me. I saw in their faces an
expression of gentle, childish pleasure, and carefree
relaxation, but no hint of generosity.

❹ This was all very well, but I was making no money, and
there was scarcely room among the crowd to swing my arm.   45
Every so often I was compelled to stop playing, and to
attempt some sort of a speech, begging the crowd to walk
up and down a little, or to draw back and reveal my hat that
was lying on the ground. A number of nearby soldiers, half
understanding what I was trying to say, began to shout out   50
instructions to the crowd on my behalf. The crowd screamed
back, telling them to be quiet and to listen to my playing. In
the meantime, nobody had moved.

❺ Presently a policeman appeared, his unbuttoned tunic
somehow in keeping with a dirty rifle slung carelessly over   55
his shoulder. He asked to see my licence. He gave it a
sleepy glance. Then, shifting his rifle to the other shoulder,
he hooked my hat on to the toe of his boot, tossed it high
in the air, caught it, shook it, and turned to the crowd with
anger on his face. 'Look, not even half a peseta. Either pay   60
or go.' Turning to me he said, 'Now, please continue.'
Giggling uneasily, the crowd backed away. There was a tinkle
of a solitary coin on the pavement. The policeman picked it
up, dropped it into the hat, and handed it to me with a
polite bow. My career as a violin player in the streets of   65
Valladolid had begun.

Now here is the summary question set on the text:

The author describes his experiences in playing his violin in Valladolid, a city in Spain, and how the people there reacted to his playing.

Using your own words as far as possible, summarise from the text what he had to do before he started playing, how people reacted to him, and what encouraged him to go on.

Your summary, which must be in continuous writing (*not note form*), must not be longer than 160 words, including the opening 10 words given below.

Begin your summary as follows:

To play for money I needed a licence and so...

A list of the content points for this summary now follows.

Don't peep at them yet! Do your own version and then see how many content points you got right.

	Line no.
Para 1	
1. I went to the city hall	2–3
2. I was met by a queue of people waiting there	6–7
3. I hurried past them	9
4. I opened the first door I came to	9–10
Para 2	
5. and was faced by a city magistrate	11
6. he took no notice of me at first	14–15

	Line No.
Para 2	
7. I told him what I wanted/asked for a licence to play	19–20
8. in the end he gave me a licence	22–23
Para 3	
9. I bought a new straw hat	26
10. and fetched my violin from my lodgings	27–28
11. and began to play in a busy lane	29–30
12. having placed my hat on the ground	29
13. people crowded round me in silence	35–36
14. they kept on treading on my hat	37
15. I kept on pushing it forward for their contributions	38–39
16. but they gave me no money	39
17. I went and played somewhere else	39–40
18. the crowd followed	41
19. but they wouldn't give me anything/were not feeling generous	43
Para 4	
20. I begged them to keep clear of my hat	47–48
21. and some soldiers urged them to as well	49–51
Para 5	
22. then a policeman asked me for my licence	54–56
23. and criticised the crowd for not giving me anything	60–61
24. finally someone tossed a coin on the pavement for me	62–63

Now here is a finished version of the summary. To help you recognise the content points, the numbers assigned to them are inserted against the points in the summary.

To play for money I needed a licence and so I went to the city hall (1). Scurrying past (3) a queue of locals there (2), I opened the first door I saw (4). The magistrate inside ignored me (6) until I told him what I wanted (7). Then he wrote me out a licence (8). Off I went to my lodgings for my violin (10), having bought a new straw hat on the way (9). Finding a busy lane, I put down my hat (12) and began playing (11). People gathered round quietly (13), meanwhile trampling on my hat (14) which I kept pushing towards them for money (15), to no avail (16). As soon as I went to play elsewhere (17), round they came again (18), but still gave me nothing (19). I kept pleading with them to mind my hat (20) and some soldiers joined in with my pleas (21). A policeman now arrived. Asking to see my licence (22), he then rebuked the bystanders for being mean (23). Finally someone threw a coin on the pavement (24).

(158 words)

Frequently asked questions

Question

Will I be penalised if my summary has more words than the number of words indicated in the rubric?

Answer

The examiner will not deduct marks for a summary which exceeds the number of words indicated in the rubric.

However, the examiner will put a line through the excess words and not even read them. Thus you will have penalised yourself. Any excess content points will be given no credit whatsoever. There is therefore no need for further penalty from the examiner.

Question

Will I be penalised if my summary is too short?

Answer

Yes. But again, it will be a case of your penalising yourself. If the rubric specifies 160 words as the maximum, you should write around 135 words, including the opening 10 words supplied, but no fewer. If you write fewer words than this you will find it difficult to include sufficient content points. It can be difficult enough to squeeze all 15 content points into around 135 words!

Besides, a short answer will not be entitled to full credit for style. Answers which fall short by 25 words (or more) of the maximum specified in the rubric cannot be considered for the full mark for style.

Question

Will the examiner count the number of words I have written?

Answer

Yes. All summaries are checked for the number of words used. Examiners make sure that a rubric instruction such as 'not more than 160 words' is strictly adhered to. The only way they can be sure is by counting the words used.

Question

Can I save on words by contracting words, e.g. by using 'don't' instead of 'do not'?

Answer

No. The examiner will count 'don't' as two words, and so you gain nothing. Remember that summary writing is a piece of formal prose, and contractions such as 'don't' have no place in it; they belong to a more informal style.

Question

Will I be penalised if I forget to indicate on my script the number of words I have used?

Answer

No. Nevertheless, you will want to know for yourself how many words are in your summary so that you write neither too short nor too long a summary. Therefore it is good practice to write down the number of words you have used.

Question

Will I be penalised if I don't use the opening 10 words supplied in the question?

Answer

No. However, you will again penalise yourself. The opening 10 words are specifically designed to lead you into the first available content point. Also, if you do not use them, the examiner will count the first word of your summary as number 11, so you have not gained an extra 10 words for yourself!

Question

Does it matter whether my summary is in one single paragraph or several?

Answer

Unless the rubric specifies a particular number of paragraphs for your summary – which is rather unusual – you may write more than one if you wish. However, the nature of the task, and the relatively short run of words required, mean that for practical purposes you will probably need only one paragraph.

Question

Will I get credit for an answer in note form?

Answer

Your summary is marked for both content and style. If within such an answer you have made content points in full, you will gain marks for them in the normal way. However, you will automatically gain no marks for style. Answers in note form are not a good idea!

Question

If the rubric specifies that my summary should be written in the first person (i.e. 'I' and 'we' instead of 'she'/'he'/'they') will I be penalised if I forget to do so?

Answer

There is no set penalty for this error. Nevertheless, if you forget to obey the rubric in this instruction, it is taken into account when the style of your summary is assessed. Usually, it counts as a single error in your writing; you won't be penalised for the same error every time! However, it is an error, and it always pays to obey the rubric.

Unit 4 — Further practice

In this chapter there are more passages that will enable you to practise the summary skills you have been acquiring. There are six passages in all, and in each case the summary question follows. You are advised to work through them in the order in which they are set. Model answers for each passage follow at the end of the chapter. Try not to peep at the model answers first!

Exercise 1

The following passage (of around 230 words) is an extract from a longer passage, set in Argentina, which describes a season in which giant thistles grew unusually well.

Although there were many disadvantages of the giant thistle, it is nevertheless true to say that a 'thistle year' was a blessing in some ways. Admittedly, it was an anxious year on account of the risk of fire, and a season of great apprehension, too, when reports of robberies and other violent crimes were widespread. It was especially worrying for the wives of the gauchos* who were left so much alone in their low-roofed mud houses, shut in by dense, prickly growth. But a 'thistle year' was also called a fat year, since the animals – cattle, horses, sheep and even pigs – gorged themselves on the huge leaves and soft, sweetish-tasting stems, and were in excellent condition. The only drawbacks were that the riding horses lost strength as they gained in fat, and milk did not taste nice.

The best and fattest time would come when the hardening thistles were no longer fit to eat and their shrivelling flowers began to shed their seed. The fallen seed was so abundant as to cover the ground under the dead but still standing plants. The sheep feasted on it, using their mobile and extensive upper lips like brushes to gather it into their mouths; horses gathered it in the same way. Pigs flourished on it, and it was even more important to the birds than to the wild or domestic mammals.

*gaucho is a South American cowboy.

Using your own words as far as possible, write a summary of the *advantages* of a 'thistle year'.

Your summary, which must be in continuous writing (not note form), must not be longer than 60 words, including the opening 10 words given below.

Begin your summary as follows:

A 'thistle year' brought some advantages to the people because…

Exercise 2

This passage (of around 280 words) is taken from a longer passage about the Great Wall of China. This section outlines some of the difficulties involved in the construction of the wall, and how these difficulties were overcome.

> The actual work of building the Great Wall, both in ancient times and more recently in the Ming Dynasty, is a testimony to the ingenuity of the Chinese people. The recruitment of labour was a major difficulty in undertaking such a gigantic project. In the early stages, soldiers were used to do this work, and sometimes thousands of local peasants as well as the army were forced to take part. During the reign of one emperor, over a million men were engaged in the construction of the wall. Moreover, a special penalty existed during the reign of other emperors, under which convicted criminals were made to work on the wall as a way of atoning for their crimes.
>
> The building of the Great Wall involved the untold sorrow of many families and the blood and sweat of countless labourers; some of this suffering has been immortalised in legend, literature and the theatre. Engineers had the difficult task of organising the labour forces. They divided up construction tasks among different groups; particularly large groups of workers were assigned to difficult sections of the wall's construction. Sometimes, supervision of work was done by the commanding generals in the important towns

along the border. The builders were directed mainly by military requirements, and yet the wall owes some of its beauty to these very people. For they often decorated the gateways in the wall in ways which, from the military point of view, would seem to be unnecessary. The pride of the builders themselves is shown by the inscriptions they made on some sections of the wall, showing the date of completion and their own names. The designers also enhanced the wall with sacred buildings, temples and shrines.

Using your own words as far as possible, summarise the difficulties encountered by the builders of the Great Wall, and explain how these difficulties were overcome.

Your summary, which must be in continuous writing (not note form), must not be longer than 70 words, including the opening 10 words given below.

Begin your summary as follows:

It was difficult for the builders of the Great Wall...

Exercise 3

Venice is a city built on a series of islands in a shallow lake separating the mainland of Italy from the sea. The following passage (of around 320 words) is an extract from a longer passage about the flooding of Venice. In this extract, the writer outlines the reasons why the flood happened, and explains some of the permanent damage done to the buildings of Venice.

To begin with, the maintenance of the sea walls had been neglected, and when they were most needed they collapsed. Because of the gradual melting of the ice cap at the North Pole, the level of the sea has been rising, threatening to reach the level of the streets in the city. At the same time the area of the River Po behind Venice has been sinking about ten times as fast, taking Venice with it. Some of this sinking is natural and inevitable, but it has been accelerated by the extraction of fresh water from the ground beneath Venice for use in the huge industrial development on the mainland of Italy.

This same industrial development, although bringing prosperity to neighbouring Venice, has also upset the city's defences. Industry needed land for expansion, for docks to unload raw materials, and to accommodate increasingly bigger ships. It has disturbed the level of the lake with schemes for reclaiming this land from the water, and with the cutting of new and deeper channels. The wash of its giant ships as they pass close to the city has had a destructive effect on its canals. The waste products of industry have polluted the water and its fumes the air. The flood waters contain not only sea salt, which can be damaging enough, but also chemical pollution, which is worse. The polluted water enters the structure of Venetian buildings and creeps through their walls, until they decay, and the canals that were once overlooked by some of the finest houses in Europe now run between mile after mile of rotting beauty. The polluted air attacks the stone of the city's sculpture, eating away the fine detail and then consuming the marble at an ever-increasing pace until it crumbles into dust. By the time this effect had even been noticed, much less something done about it, it was already too late to save the best of Venice's sculpture.

Using your own words as far as possible, write an account summarising not only the causes of the disastrous flood but also the permanent damage done to Venice and its buildings.

Your summary, which must be in continuous writing (not note form), must not be longer than 100 words, including the opening 10 words given below.

Begin your summary as follows:

The sea walls had not been looked after properly and…

Exercise 4

The following passage (of around 340 words) is taken from a longer passage which describes the destruction of the forests of western Brazil and the harmful results of that destruction.

The results of this destruction are becoming frighteningly obvious. The forests contain an astonishing variety of animal and plant life which is slowly but surely disappearing. One type of tree may maintain more than 400 insect species, each square kilometre of forest its own assortment of birds and mammals. The forests vanish, and with them the rich variety of their animal life and the great treasure house of plants. The scientific benefits the forests can bring are also being lost to doctors and farmers as the destruction goes on. Many of the plants contain chemicals that can help medical science and agriculture, providing new treatments for diseases or controlling insects that do immense damage to crops. Such natural chemicals are better than artificial ones, which can have dangerous effects on animals and people.

Even more alarming is the threat to the world's climate. These forests create huge volumes of clouds as the water evaporates from the great expanse of the treetops. These clouds distribute the sun's warmth round the world. The destruction of the forests would mean that the clouds would no longer form, and so the delicate balance of the world's weather systems would be very seriously upset. The actual burning of the trees accelerates the warming up of the Earth's upper atmosphere, which scientists now say will bring dramatic changes to our climate. Moreover, the blazing torches of the jungles will add to the harmful gases that cars and modern industries are pouring into the air we breathe.

The Indians who live in these forests are already victims of this destruction. Violent clashes with the new settlers and farmers have resulted in some tribes losing half their number. Newly introduced diseases, against which the Indians have no natural immunity, have also killed off many others. Again, the Indians have been compelled to live in other parts of the jungle and are suddenly deprived of a

way of life developed over many generations. They lose their will to
live along with their simple means of livelihood. Many just starve to
death.

Using your own words as far as possible, write a summary of the
harmful effects of the destruction of the forests of western Brazil.

Your summary, which should be in continuous writing (not note
form), must not be longer than 130 words, including the opening 10
words given below.

Begin your summary as follows:

The destruction of the forests has meant the disappearance of...

Exercise 5

The writer of the passage which follows (of around 620 words) has
been visiting a game reserve. He describes how he accompanies
some rangers on a hunt for elephant poachers, with unexpected
results.

Early in the morning, a convoy of trucks, keeping well apart to avoid
each other's dust, carried the rangers up onto the plateau. There
they stopped periodically to set down a section of rangers, who
immediately disappeared into scrub so thick that the vehicles
themselves had to force a passage through it. Each man carried a
rifle and a small water bottle, and each section had a radio. When
all were in position, the various sections were ready to converge on
the edge of the plateau, thereby trapping any poachers who were
between them and the steep drop down to the valley below. The
patrol I was accompanying formed into single file and set out
confidently through the thornbushes.

Suddenly, disaster struck. For most of the party, the first warning
anyone had was when the feet of the man immediately in front of
him stopped. Up ahead, the leading ranger had halted and was

looking intently to his left. A complete silence had fallen among us. Then, without a word, he turned on his heel and started to run very fast to his right. Immediately, his well-disciplined and heavily armed formation dispersed. Everyone ran as fast as he could, though where to or what from it was impossible to tell. After a few seconds, with nothing apparently behind them, they began stopping and looking back, hoping to see what it was that had caused this sudden rush.

The leading ranger had paused by this time and was pointing his rifle towards a bush from which there slowly emerged a snout with a horn on it. The ranger fired a warning shot into the ground ahead of him, raising a little puff of dust in front of the snout. At once a rhinoceros started to trot towards him. The ranger fired again, this time to kill. The only effect was to make the animal run faster. The ranger dropped his rifle and ran. Everyone ran. I dived behind a small thornbush and for five minutes I watched as the rhinoceros chased eight men around its territory. Equipment was dropped: notebooks, a box of dates, a canvas bucket, some fresh figs, items of clothing, even some of the rifles. The shortwave radio was dropped, crackling and spluttering, into a bush.

The rhinoceros cantered between the scattered rangers, the men on either side dodging from its path and firing at it, and, incidentally, towards each other as it passed. There was no shouting. The popping of the guns, the crackling of the radio, occasional sharp explosions as twigs snapped beneath boots – none of these noises broke the silence of the men's concentration. But the rhinoceros was concentrating still harder, and closer and closer came the loudest sound of all, its huffing and puffing and thumping feet.

Meanwhile, from behind my small thornbush I could see the rhinoceros in pursuit of the scattered rangers, some armed, some unarmed. Then to my horror I saw it turn and head towards my thornbush, drawn to my refuge as though by magnetism. Occasional shots from the rangers did not slow it for a moment. I decided that, contrary to popular belief, its eyesight was clearly capable of penetrating the bush; at the last moment I dodged around the far side of the thicket and ran flat out, away from the rhinoceros. I

> glanced back and saw a grey shape, by now apparently twice the size of any known rhinoceros. It turned with great nimbleness directly behind me; then I tripped headlong right in front of it, but I did not feel a thing except the thorns in my skin. The rhinoceros had decided to trample on somebody else, it seemed, and then at long last and a few metres away was shot dead.

When the author accompanied the rangers on a patrol to catch poachers, the expedition did not turn out as expected.

Using your own words as far as possible, write a summary of what the rangers and their leader did when they first set out, what they did when they were confronted by the rhinoceros, and how the author reacted to its presence.

Your summary, which must be in continuous writing (not note form), must not be longer than 160 words, including the opening 10 words given below.

Begin your summary as follows:

Early in the morning, the rangers moved off in a...

Exercise 6
The following passage (of around 700 words) describes a journey that the narrator has to make alone through difficult and sometimes dangerous terrain.

> Eventually I set off, feeling more than a little isolated. Above me towered a steep slope culminating in a sheer, grey cliff. Somehow it seemed to symbolise the task I had set myself. Elsewhere, though, there were magnificent views. The wooded areas, looking as elegant as if they had been deliberately landscaped, contrasted with the wilder scene of the hills and rivers that stretched into the distance. Only to the west was the view interrupted, by a bank of cloud. Somewhere behind it lay my goal – Mount Roraima – but not too far behind, I hoped. The nagging doubts returned.

It was time to make a start but, having expected to be flown straight to the village, I was badly overloaded with presents which I had brought for the local people, among them some bulky hammocks and blankets. I picked out the essentials for my journey – compass, map, sleeping bag, torch and camera, along with the only food I had with me, a bunch of bananas. I hid everything else carefully in a dense thicket and then, with my compass in my hand, set off into woodland, towards the mountain.

There was a track, but it kept on dividing. Part of my mind had to keep concentrating on which path to follow, the other part wandered in a way that had not been possible for some time. At long last the labours and mental stress of the last three months were behind me. Now that there was no need to plan, discuss, argue or talk, my step lightened and began to quicken as I journeyed on through this silent place. Insects buzzed around my head, and the hot sun beat down on the hard, burnt ground. Apart from the hum of insect life and occasional stirrings and rustlings in the undergrowth, an overpowering silence lay over the landscape. It was lonely – and a little frightening.

Towards evening I reached a thick belt of jungle. A glance at my map showed me that it marked one of the rivers I had to cross. I chose a flat piece of ground, hacked up some of the hard sandy earth to make it softer to lie on, and laid my sleeping bag over the top. After eating a couple of bananas I settled down and went to sleep. I slept fitfully. Once I heard the gruff barking of some wild animal, and a little later a few drops of rain fell. Finally, I awoke and, warmed by the first rays of the sun, I set out for the river marked on my map, looking forward to a cool drink after some thirteen hours without any water. Suddenly I saw the river, yet I was still separated from it by a steep and densely overgrown slope. The jungle, too, on the far bank, looked impenetrable and forbidding.

At last I found a track which led down to the water's edge and I scrambled down it. I waded across the river, gulping down handfuls of water as I did so. Depositing everything on the far bank, I dived back into the river for a very refreshing and welcome swim. As I emerged, the dark stretch of jungle confronted me. In its depths a bell-bird was calling monotonously. The solitude almost seduced me; I could gladly have stayed there, avoiding the long journey ahead, but I had to continue. Following the faint track through the dense, gloomy undergrowth meant that I took several wrong turns, until at last I burst into the sunlight again. Here in open country the path was clear and easy to follow. It went winding up along a narrow ridge, gaining height all the time. Then Mount Roraima came into view. Even so I could not yet make out the summit. I began to wonder whether I could reach the foot of the mountain before nightfall.

Jungle once more shrouded the path I was following. I plunged into the undergrowth, grateful that the path was still visible, but instead of simply having to put one foot in front of the other in order to go forward, I had to keep on climbing. Moreover, an ominous fog was beginning to gather and it was getting dark.

Much of the author's journey was difficult and worrying.

Using your own words as far as possible, summarise these difficulties and worries.

Your summary, which must be in continuous writing (not note form), must not be longer than 160 words, including the opening 10 words given below.

Begin your summary as follows:

As soon as I set off, I began to feel...

The model answers for the summary passages you have been working on follow below. They are in the same order as that of the passages.

Exercise 1   Model Answer

A 'thistle year' brought some advantages to the people because the thistles provided abundant food for their animals, thus keeping them very healthy. Later, when the seed fell from the thistles and covered the ground, it became yet another banquet for sheep, horses and pigs, and, even more importantly, for birds.   (51 words)

Exercise 2   Model Answer

It was difficult for the builders of the Great Wall to find enough workers, and so they coerced soldiers and people from the surrounding countryside. In addition, convicts were drafted in, as an alternative to prison. The difficult job of organising the huge numbers of workers fell to engineers, who assigned work to particular groups depending on their size. Building was overseen by army generals in key border towns.   (69 words)

Exercise 3   Model Answer

The sea walls had not been looked after properly and gave way. Melting ice at the North Pole has raised the sea, and the land behind Venice has been sinking, causing Venice to sink. Industry removes water from underneath Venice and, in its reclamation of land, cuts deeper channels in the lake, thus upsetting its depth. Waves from ships damage canals, while industry dirties water with its waste and the air with its fumes. Flood water contains damaging salt and chemicals. Polluted water causes buildings to rot away, and polluted air eats away stonework, until it disintegrates.   (97 words)

Exercise 4   Model Answer

The destruction of forests has meant the disappearance of a rich
selection of animals and plants. Moreover, medicine and farming
suffer from the loss of natural, harmless chemicals found in these
plants. The world's weather patterns are also endangered because,
since clouds cease to form, solar heat is no longer spread around
the earth. When trees burn, this speeds up the rising temperature of
the earth's upper atmosphere; thus another noticeable change to
the climate occurs. Furthermore, blazing trees add to toxic fumes
from cars and industry. Indians are killed by new jungle inhabitants,
or die of new diseases they transmit. Sometimes they are forced to
live elsewhere in the jungle and are barred from their traditional way
of life. They no longer wish to live; many die of starvation.

(130 words)

Exercise 5   Model Answer

Early in the morning, the rangers moved off in a group of vehicles
which took them on to the plateau and dropped them off at
intervals. They hurried into the scrub and prepared to meet up on
the edge of the plateau to trap poachers. My patrol set off through
the bushes. The leading ranger suddenly stopped and looked hard
to his left. Everyone was quiet, and, when he ran off in the opposite
direction, we scattered. When we looked back, we saw the leader
aiming his rifle at a bush, firing a warning shot. When a rhinoceros
appeared, he fired again, trying to kill it. Throwing down his rifle, he
ran. We all ran. I hid behind a bush, watching the rhinoceros
pursuing rangers, who dropped equipment and dodged it, firing at it.
I was terrified when it charged towards my hideout, and darted out,
falling in front of it. However, just at that moment, it was killed.

(159 words)

Exercise 6   Model Answer

As soon as I set off, I began to feel all alone. I was confronted by an almost vertical cliff, which seemed to represent the difficult job before me. Because Mount Roraima was hidden by cloud, I had further misgivings. Moreover, my food supply was limited. The path I was on kept splitting, making careful thinking necessary; it was very hot and the silence frightened me. I had to lie on hard ground, which interrupted my sleep. For a long time I had not had a drink, yet an overgrown bank lay between me and the river, while the jungle on the other side seemed threatening. I had to struggle to the river. In addition, the path on the other side was difficult to see, causing me to go often in the wrong direction. I worried that I might not reach Mount Roraima before it was dark. The track went uphill, and further problems were mist and falling darkness.   (159 words)